Hello!
This is MESSAGE...

Through the year with the
MESSAGE Christian Telephone Service

 The Bible Reading Fellowship

Text copyright © MESSAGE 1994

Published jointly by
The Bible Reading Fellowship
Peter's Way, Sandy Lane West, Oxford OX4 5HG
and
MESSAGE Christian Telephone Service
6 Darnley Road, Woodford Green, Essex IG8 9HU

ISBN 0 7459 3089 1

First edition 1994
All rights reserved

A catalogue record for this book is available
from the British Library

All royalties from the sales of this book
go towards the work of MESSAGE

Typeset and prepared in Great Britain
by Index Print, Colchester, Essex

Printed and bound in Malta

INTRODUCTION

by the Rt Revd Michael E Vickers, Bishop of Colchester
National Chairman of MESSAGE

25 years ago the sister of a future Archbishop of Canterbury caught a vision. In that vision Norah Coggan saw a network of Centres across the nation providing people with a "Dial and Listen" Christian telephone service. By the simplest of means it would be possible to hear local down-to-earth Christians talking about their faith and relating it to everyday life.

That vision became a reality although some corners of the nation have yet to be reached. The network became known as MESSAGE and over the years since 1969 it has been able to help half a million callers. Its daily 2-minute messages have come from local people of various Christian traditions working together. They have spoken from their own immediate experience, from an awareness of human anxieties or dilemmas and from a firm reliance upon the word of God in the Bible.

Members of MESSAGE have asked themselves how we might mark our silver jubilee and at the same time provide something of really practical use. This book is the result. It contains a selection from a cross-section of daily messages over the years, 100 in all, from MESSAGE Centres as far apart as York and Jersey. They have been grouped to follow the seasons of the year and the great Christian festivals and anniversaries. With each message go suggested Bible readings and a prayer. The prayers have been written by leaders from several different branches of the Christian Church, reflecting the totally ecumenical basis of MESSAGE. So you have here a valuable source of inspiration, a series of subjects for thought and meditation and a possible starting point and incentive for personal prayer. It is also ideal as a resource book for those called on to lead group devotions. The comprehensive index under Scriptural and topic headings will be very helpful in this respect.

This is a book that is meant to be handled, and in its handling there will be fitting celebration of 25 years of ministry and sharing by the people who founded MESSAGE and those who have carried on the work.

+ Michael Colchester

A MESSAGE FROM THE
ARCHBISHOP OF CANTERBURY

As President of MESSAGE, I warmly congratulate all those who have had a part to play in writing and transmitting these messages or who have been involved in the production of this book. The Good News that Jesus came to bring needs to be heard by many today. I pray that God will continue to use MESSAGE to bring that Good News to many.

+ George Carey

EDITOR'S PREFACE

This book provides rich fare and may cause indigestion if swallowed in haste. It is the product of many minds, many hearts, many prayers. Though modest in size its scope is broad. 'Life's rich pattern', the comings and goings, the ups and downs of daily routine, the variety of work and leisure, high days and holidays: all of this recognisable, familiar world appears somehow new and different as Christians from a wide range of backgrounds and traditions talk about how it looks to them. They share their personal experiences and their personal faith. Simply, unpretentiously, with humour and freshness, without dogma. They are people who have caught glimpses of the Christian God but go on looking. They are people who have found some answers but aren't afraid of asking more questions. The prayers echo this, and coming as they do from leading Christians of today, they are remarkable for their mood of humble searching. What's more, I am confident readers will be unable to identify which were written by, say, a Salvation Army Commissioner, or a Franciscan friar or an Anglican bishop. I appreciate very much the depth and detail of the drawings, saying so clearly, without words, how full of God is the everyday landscape of daily living.

I settled for a calendar year - January to December - as the framework for the book because I was going round in circles trying unsuccessfully to decide on the beginning of 'the Christian year'. Should it start with Christmas? The birth of Christ? Or, just as reasonably, with the cross, Good Friday? Or Easter Day? Or Pentecost? You emerge from the book with an even stronger conviction than before that every day, today!, is the beginning of the New Year.

One regret, and it's an entirely appropriate regret: as anyone knows who has ever phoned MESSAGE, it isn't just the words that you hear, it's the voice that is saying them and the person the voice reveals. That's something I can't transfer to the printed page. But of course, away from the two-minute stopwatch, we had time to search out two hundred different Scripture readings to complement the message-texts.

I close with a personal thank you to all who have helped me to produce this book, and a warm welcome to all readers:

Hello! This is MESSAGE... the Christian Telephone Service.

Diana Newlands

CONTENTS

ACKNOWLEDGEMENTS

The National Committee of MESSAGE would like to thank :

For providing the message scripts:

the MESSAGE Centres in

Ashford	01233 636981	Huntingdon	01480 450088
Brentwood	01277 213141	Redbridge	0181-514 8000
Cambridge	01223 61010	Sheffield	0114-270 0555
Eastleigh	01703 614574	Southend	01702 344255
Hove	01273 721666	York	01904 795555

and Jersey 1884 (only available from within Jersey)

for contributing the prayers:

Andrea Adams	Moderator of the Council for World Mission and President of the Congregational Federation
Revd Chris Bard	Religious Producer for Radio Essex and Vicar of Epping Upland in the Diocese of Chelmsford
Bishop Geoffrey Birtill	Bishop in the Moravian Church. Member of the Provincial Board and part-time minister of the Moravian Church in Chelsea
Revd David Coffey	General Secretary of the Baptist Union of Great Britain
Revd Dr Donald English	General Secretary of the Methodist Church, Home Mission Division
Jackie Hawkins	Executive Editor of *The Way* journals of spirituality
Fr Patrick Lonsdale	Brother Guardian of Forest Gate Friary, East London. Secretary of the Province for the Franciscan Order in Great Britain
Commissioner Dinsdale Pender	Territorial Commander, Salvation Army, United Kingdom Territory
Bishop John V. Taylor	Former Bishop of Winchester

for contributing suggestions for Bible readings:

Philip Bayliss, Candy Claridge, Joan Davison, Jean and Harry Gill, Michael Graves, Graham Hardwick, Diana Hargreaves, David Hatch, Kathy Jacob, Margaret Simmonds, all of whom are involved, each in a different way, with the MESSAGE service.

for contributing the illustrations:

Peter Butler and Helena Gardner

for supervising the typesetting, artwork and production:

Howard Gardner and Sarah Mills at Index Print

for all their help and ideas in getting this book published:

The Bible Reading Fellowship

and for selecting, arranging and editing the book's contents:

Diana Newlands

OPENING
MESSAGES

JESUS: GOD'S MESSAGE

I wonder what kind of picture the word 'message' conveys to you. A short, snappy note of very little consequence maybe. Just a brief communication like "Gone to Jane's, be back at 4." But some messages are much more important and have far-reaching effects if they are ignored : "S.O.S." for example. Even though it is very short it is a real cry for help and is often a matter of life or death. In any message at least two people are involved, the sender and the receiver, and the one wishes to convey some kind of information to the other. We Christians believe that when God wanted to communicate with his people on earth, he sent Jesus to be this 'word' or 'message' to mankind. John chapter 1 verse 14 tells us: "The Word became flesh and dwelt among us." The Christian message is one of hope in this troubled world. When Jesus, the Son of God, came to live among us, sharing our problems, he showed us more clearly than any written or spoken message that God cares deeply about us. In his teaching, his example, his death and his resurrection, he demonstrated the love, the power and the forgiveness of God. He still offers that love, that power and that forgiveness to us all.

> **Forgive me, Lord God,**
> **for thinking you are unreal or indifferent.**
> **Perhaps you have spoken to me often in the past**
> **and I never recognized that it was your voice.**
> **Help me to listen and to understand**
> **what you are saying.**
>
> *Amen*

For further reading

Luke 15:11-24   The love and forgiveness of God
Romans 10:11-17   Faith comes from hearing the message

PERSONALLY RECOMMENDED

Do you take any notice of all those advertisements on television and in the newspapers? I am sure many of us don't. But suppose a good friend rang up and urged us to try a particular product because they had found it very effective? I suspect that even those of us who usually ignore advertisements in the media would be likely to give it a try. And in a way, that's what MESSAGE is like. Every day on this number there is a new message. The speakers are all local Christians. Some may even be neighbours of yours. Ordinary people who have faced problems in life and have found help through faith in God, our creator; who have been conscious of his presence when the going seemed hard; and who have proved for themselves that his love is a love that never lets go. There is no anxiety too trivial to be shared with him in prayer and no problem too difficult to handle with his help. St. Paul wrote these words when he himself was enduring considerable suffering: "I am convinced that nothing can separate us from the love of God." May God bless you and meet your need to-day.

> Dear God, I am ashamed to think
>   that your love has always been there
>   yet I have ignored it.
> Your hand was held out to help me
>   and I wouldn't take it.
> Forgive my ingratitude and help me
>   to recognize your presence today.
>   *Amen.*

For further reading

John 1:35-46   Gossiping the Good News
1 John 1:1-4   What we ourselves have seen and heard,
  we now proclaim to you

AN INVITATION TO GOD'S PARTY

I wonder if you have ever almost shied away from 'religious' things because you felt they were dull, flat, uninteresting? I must confess I have. There's something radically wrong if this happens. For the facts about God and about Jesus Christ are exciting, stimulating, thrilling. So we must have got hold of the wrong end of the stick. One of to-day's writers puts it like this: "Somehow we have managed the incredible, we have somehow made Jesus dull. What hundreds of ordinary Galileans walked ten miles and missed their lunch to hear, we have turned into something that the average Englishman would walk ten miles and miss his lunch to escape!" The same writer also says: "What Jesus brings is not moral teaching but good news. He comes with the news of a Kingdom where life is free and men are whole. He comes with an invitation to God's party, to join the laughter of the angels, and the song of the morning stars." Jesus himself knew that he was bringing men quite a different quality of living. He expressed it plainly when he said: "I have come that men may have life, and may have it in all its fullness." (John 10v10) So many of us just 'exist', and turn away from what we think is 'dull', when the fact of the matter is that real living contact with the living Christ cannot but bring life, and hope. For the present and right on into the next world.

Lord Jesus Christ,
    if it is true that you are alive in some way I do not understand,
    then please bring me to life in a way that hasn't yet happened,
    so that I can begin to recognize your reality and respond to it.
                                    Amen.

For further reading

Matthew 13:44-46   The sheer joy of discovering the kingdom
Mark 2:1-12   We've never seen anything like this!

THE NEW YEAR

LOVE WITHOUT LIMITS

Hello, and welcome to MESSAGE, and welcome to the New Year! Are you like me? I find the New Year is a good time for clearing out cupboards, getting rid of useless clutter that's only making it hard to get at the things I really want. It's not easy in the space of two minutes, but if I were trying to do the same for my Christian faith, seeing what's really essential and worth hanging on to, I'd say: my faith is NOT about MY struggles to pray, MY efforts to lead a better life and love my neighbour and turn the other cheek and go the second mile. My faith IS about the fact that GOD has taken action: he has done everything that was necessary to fetch me back to him. He came to this earth in the person of Jesus and said: "Look, this is what I'm like. Can't you see?" Mixing in close friendship with all kinds of people. Not checking up first on what they believed or what their father did for a living. Love without limits. Serving others as a slave. Washing their smelly feet before supper. Forgiving even those who were nailing him to the cross. This is the Christian God. God in the everyday situations of life. God closer than breathing. God in everyone we meet. God saying to us: "Whenever you listen to a grieving friend or visit a lonely widow or feed a hungry child, you're doing it for me." You can believe it or not. But a New Year is as good a time as any to give it another hearing. May God bless you, and me, and make himself plain to us in the events of to-day.

> **Dear Lord, even at New Year**
> **it can be difficult to see our usual,**
> **humdrum life with fresh eyes.**
> **Through your Spirit, give me new energy to**
> **grasp the transforming message of your love**
> **for us, by following the example of Jesus,**
> **seeing others as he did,**
> **and responding to them in love.**
>
> *Amen.*

For further reading

John 3:16-17   God so loved the world...
Matthew 25:31-40   ...you did it for me

NEWNESS OF LIFE

A new year! Did you know that the most popular word in advertising is 'new'? A new whiteness, a new ingredient, a new sound. Have a glance at your bathroom shelf, at all the aftershaves, bath oils and beauty lotions that multiplied there at Christmas, and see what zest and fitness you should be exhibiting, according to the blurb on the bottles. What 'newness of life'! The same words St. Paul used to describe the gift that Jesus gives to his followers. Well, it's hardly surprising that many people dismiss such an idea lightly when the same can be claimed of a bath cube! But what if it should be true, as many Christians confirm? (And they're not getting commission on sales!) What sort of newness can it be? Well, I suppose that anyone who has experienced deep human love will know how different the world looks in the light of such love. And how much more astonishing the discovery that God himself knows, understands and loves us utterly. In the light of that love, the whole of eternity looks different. Everything is new. It's a message to marvel at!

> We're supposed to be living advertisements for
>   you, Lord, aren't we?
> Help me to steer well clear of clever blurb that
>   just misleads people.
> It would be better if I could trust more
>   completely in your love for me and then,
>   in the security of that,
>   learn to share it more generously.
>
>   *Amen.*

For further reading
2 Corinthians 5:17   A new person
Revelation 21:1-5   A new heaven and a new earth

A CLEAN SHEET

There seems to be a tremendous attraction for all of us in the idea of something new. And I must admit that, even after years of breaking New Year's resolutions I still get excited about beginning a new year. Turning over a new leaf, quite literally, in the diary. But perhaps, like me, you've already made a hash of things even this early in January. Said things you wish you hadn't said, and all that. And like me thinking: "So much for my clean sheet!" Funnily enough, all this seems to lie right at the heart of the Christian faith. Even St. Paul was frustrated that, as he put it, "the good that I want to do is exactly what I end up not doing, and I don't seem to be able to get any better." So what is the answer? You often hear Christians talking about good news. And the good news announced by Jesus is that on any day at any time we can start all over again with a completely clean sheet. New people altogether really, because the past is completely forgiven. Mind you, there is one condition: we also have to let go of hard feelings against people who may have hurt us. What a different world this would be, this New Year, if that law of practical peacemaking were kept. We at least can make it our first, new, New Year's resolution!

> **Deepen my belief, Lord, that through Jesus all**
> **my past wrongdoing is forgiven.**
> **Through this experience may I learn to forgive**
> **others with generosity of heart, and go**
> **forward in life with renewed and certain**
> **hope.**
>
> *Amen.*

For further reading

Matthew 5:1-24   Tough words about practical peacemaking
(and other things!)
1 John 2:7-11   A new commandment

A FRESH START

I imagine St. Peter would have been the sort to make New Year's resolutions... and then break them, just like us. When Jesus first met him he was called Simon. As a fisherman, Simon was probably quite good. On shore, he was a walking disaster area. The sort of person who opens his mouth and puts his foot in it. Says what he thinks, without stopping to think first, argues, squabbles, pokes his nose into other people's business, treads on people's toes, blows hot and cold, impetuous, unreliable. Yet this was the man Jesus nicknamed Peter, Rocky, telling him he'd be the firm foundation for the Church. He could see Peter blundering along his disastrous way, knew he'd run into trouble, knew too that he had the strength to learn from failure and despair, to become a real rock. Peter even denied knowing Jesus. He was confused and frightened. And that betrayal was hard to forgive...hardest for Peter to forgive himself. But Jesus gave Peter another chance to declare his love; three chances in fact, as he had denied him three times. What's more, Jesus entrusted him with work to do. Peter served Jesus faithfully, and probably died for his loyalty. Jesus gave Peter a fresh start, and Peter justified his trust. That same offer of forgiveness and a new beginning can be ours, too.

> Lord, how hard it is to believe that you love me
>   completely and unconditionally, despite the
>   times I let you down.
> Through this compassion, help me to love
>   myself, accepting my limitations as you do,
>   and to persevere in my longing to follow you,
>   knowing you have complete confidence in
>   me.
>
> *Amen.*

For further reading
Matthew 16:13-19   Peter, the man of vision
John 21:15-19   Peter, the loving disciple

Hello! This is MESSAGE...

JANUARY
AND
FEBRUARY

THAT 'AFTER CHRISTMAS' FEELING

Do you enjoy feeling 'Christmassy'? Most people do, don't they? A delightful mixture of friendliness, goodwill, bright colours and lights and sounds and a touch of magical mystery as well. But what about that 'after Christmas' feeling? Oh dear, I don't know about you but the very word 'January' makes me feel bleak and dismal. But it shouldn't, of course. Not for that reason anyway. After all, we don't know for sure what month Jesus was born in. All we know is that he was born, at some lovely moment around 2000 years ago! Who knows, perhaps it was in the middle of January! Whenever it was, the world was changed for ever. From that moment, the truth is that Jesus is in our world, at Christmas and throughout the year. Christians can draw on that joy at any time. Any day can, and should, be Christmas for the Christian. Perhaps we should remind ourselves of the wonder and joy of Christ's birth every morning of our lives. Some words from a well-known Christmas carol might help us:

'O holy child of Bethlehem, descend to us, we pray.
Cast out our sin and enter in, be born in us to-day.'

**Lord Jesus, we have been remembering in a
special way your birth among us.
May the joy of this season be an ever-present
reality in our lives,
and sustain us through the coming year.**
Amen.

For further reading

Luke 1:46-55   My spirit rejoices in God, my Saviour
John 1:10-14   We have seen his glory

A DAY AT A TIME

My word, the Christmas turkey is still on the table when our television screens are blitzed with holiday adverts and brochures, enticing us to book that dream holiday in the Canaries. And as 'Auld Lang Syne' is still being sung, shops are rearranging their windows for Easter eggs. We'll soon be buying Valentine cards in October and sandals in December! It seems that the world has gone mad. And often we think and fret about next week, next month; where will I be next year? Our Lord was concerned that we should enjoy one day at a time and receive it as a gift from God. "Don't worry about tomorrow," he said to the crowds, "for tomorrow will worry about itself. Each day has enough troubles of its own." We read that Jesus rose early and lived life to the full, not taking time to look behind him or in front, although he knew what lay ahead. The hour of the cross was approaching fast and Jesus treasured every moment: using time, not as an enemy but as a friend, to love and to serve and to share all he had. Let's give thanks to God for each new day. Let's wake up to see 'today' as a new beginning, a day of opportunity to put things right that are wrong, to love and serve our neighbour and to seek God's blessing in every situation.

> **Lord Jesus, I thank you for this day,**
> **for this moment.**
> **When I am anxious about the future,**
> **remind me to place all my trust in you.**
> *Amen.*

For further reading

Matthew 6:24-34   Don't worry about tomorrow
Psalm 89:1-2, 15-18   Living in the light of God's kindness

23

NO-ONE ELSE QUITE LIKE YOU

Just recently an elderly lady I know was feeling particularly low-spirited and despondent. She felt neglected and put aside. I happened to say to her, "Yet you are very special!" She asked me what I meant and I said, "Because God made you. He couldn't resist creating you to be the person you are." She brightened up a bit and said, "I hadn't thought of that." Perhaps we all need to think of that! Especially these days when we can feel that we are just another number on a computer. Or useless, because we've been made redundant. But to God, each one of us is unique. There is no-one else quite like you. We're each a one-off design with no imitations and therefore very precious. Every creator at a human level, musician, poet, fashion designer and so on, has a special affection for what he or she has created. How much more true this is of God, whose capacity to love and care for us goes far beyond our greatest imaginings. In fact, we mean so much to God, that he allowed his son, Jesus, to die, so that, by raising him to life again, after the crucifixion, he could show us there are no limits to his love and the power of his love. And he wants to do for us what he did for Jesus because he can't bear the idea of losing us in a mortal death. Jesus expressed it in a very entertaining way when he said, "Indeed, the very hairs of your head are all numbered!"

Heavenly Father,
you know me through and through,
and you love me more than I can say.
Let me delight in this truth,
through Jesus your Son.

Amen.

For further reading

Psalm 139:1-6, 13-18 God knows everything about me...
Matthew 10:29-31 ...and still thinks I'm worth a lot!

A LOT OF COLD DAMP WEATHER

I don't know about you but I always find this time of the year rather depressing. The celebrations of Christmas and the New Year are over, and there seems to be a lot of cold damp weather to come before the Spring. Even so, we never doubt that Spring will come, though I suppose it would be difficult to prove that it will. It always has in the past, and we have experienced it personally so many times that we take it for granted. Nevertheless, it is a miracle to me, this annual rebirth of life that bursts upon us with the first snowdrop. Looking forward to it keeps me going. Another thing I look forward to at this time of year is Easter, the high point of the Christian year, when we celebrate the greatest miracle of all time, the death and resurrection of Jesus. The resurrection of Jesus is another fact experienced personally by hundreds of thousands of people, and millions more have also come to know the truth of that amazing promise he made, recorded in the last verse of Matthew's gospel: "I am with you always, to the end of time." He is alive to-day, close to us, even listening to this conversation. He stands at the door knocking and if we want to let him into our lives, it's just a simple matter of opening the door and inviting him in.

> Father, I thank you for all the signs of life and
> goodness that show through,
> even on the darkest days.
> Strengthen my faith in Jesus your Son,
> and renew my hope and confidence.
> Through Christ our Lord.
>
> *Amen*

For further reading

Genesis 8:14-22   We never doubt that Spring will come
Acts 2:22-32   Jesus has been raised to life

SUNSHINE ON A WINTRY DAY

Hi there. What's the first thing people talk about when you meet in a London suburban street in January? Ten to one it'll be the weather. Oddly enough, there's practically no mention of the weather in the Bible. Goodness knows why! One of the most famous stories Jesus ever told was about the prodigal son who went off and wasted his entire inheritance, before coming to his senses and returning home, thoroughly ashamed of himself. And how did his father react? It really shakes you, what he did. Not like fathers we might imagine. No time to grab a sunhat or even an umbrella! He just fell out of the house and ran to meet him. No questions. No reprimands. No anger. Just joy and celebration. He got right to the heart of what really matters. His son had been lost but now he was found. He had been as good as dead, but now he could start living again. This is the picture we have in the Bible of how God feels about us, his silly wandering children, when we say from our hearts, "Oh God, help me, get me back on the right track!" And it's a picture to bring the sunshine of Summer right into the heart of a wintry day.

> Father, I bless you for this image of your love
>   in the parables of Jesus.
> However much I have failed through human
>   weakness,
>   you are always ready to forgive and heal.
> Let me never stray from your goodness again.
> I ask this in Jesus' name.
>
> *Amen.*

For further reading

Luke 15:1-10   The angels throw a party
Titus 3:3-7   We went astray; God brought us back

SPRING

PRUNING HURTS!

Spring is a busy time in the garden. There is so much to be done. Before we can even attempt to think of new growth, we have to prepare the ground by weeding, and there is cutting back - pruning - to be done. It is only by thinning out the shrubs and getting rid of those invasive weeds that seem to come back year after year that we can make room for those new annual seedlings. Pruning is such a violent thing to do to a plant. Reducing it to a fraction of itself, cutting off seemingly healthy branches. But after a month or so, once the new growth starts, what a difference it makes. The plant is stronger and healthier than ever. I've had to do quite a bit of pruning in my own life in the past few weeks, none of it by choice. It hasn't been a pleasant experience. We are all a bit reluctant to cut back the familiar and embark on new growth in a different direction. But we do all need to unclog our lives, remove the weeds, if you like, and do the occasional pruning, to reassess where God is leading us. Jesus said: "I am the real vine and my father is the gardener. He breaks off every branch in me that does not bear fruit and he prunes every branch that does bear fruit, so that it will be clean and bear more fruit." Regular pruning of the roses is an easy task compared to the one of looking again at our own lives for the weeds and straggling branches.

> Lord, I do want to grow into a more whole and useful
>   person for you.
> I know that some of that will happen as I develop under
>   the influence of your Holy Spirit, and I thank you for
>   that.
> Help me also to be ready for those places where things
>   need to be pruned from my life, taken away because
>   they are a hindrance to my growth, or because I no
>   longer need them.
> Then let me grow even more strongly for you, through
>   Jesus Christ Our Lord.
>
> *Amen*

For further reading

Matthew 12:33-35   You can tell a tree by its fruit
John 15:1-8   A branch cannot bear fruit by itself

HEALTHY SOIL

I have been thinking about these words lately: "The earth is the Lord's and the fullness thereof." Possibly it's because the Spring bulbs are starting to appear. Planting bulbs brings us into close contact with the soil, and it set me thinking. To us ordinary folk soil means very little. In fact we used to call it dirt. But we have now learned to respect it and realise that it can mean life to us, if it is cultivated properly. I would change the word 'fullness' to 'miracle' "The earth is the Lord's and the miracle thereof." Surely that's what it is when we remember that it produces huge trees and tiny flowers, and vegetables too numerous to mention, wheat for our bread and fruits for our delight. Yes, soil is a miracle that we depend on. It's true, it has to be cared for and fed, and only by putting back what has been used up can we keep it healthy. I think we are all like soil. Every one of us has the ability to grow something that will benefit others and make the world a happier place. We let weeds and thistles grow in our life by wrong actions and unkind thoughts and then it's just a barren land. But if our heart is renewed and purified by Jesus, then we shall bear what St. Paul called the fruits of the Spirit: love, joy, peace.

> **Oh God, I learned to walk and talk because you had
>   built within me the desire and the impetus so to do.
> I know that under the Spirit I am the soil in which you
>   wish to grow the fruit of the Spirit.
> Please help me to turn my back on all that is bad growth,
>   to be wide open to all the good growing that is
>   possible, so that my life may be as near to being a
>   beautiful garden for you as is possible, through Jesus
> Christ Our Lord.**
>
> *Amen*

For further reading
Psalm 24:1-6   God's earth, and those who inhabit it
Mark 4:26-29   The mystery of growth

ALL CHANGE!

Haven't things changed! People are often looking back and talking about the good old days', and how things used to be. All around us is change. Places being demolished. New buildings going up. New roads being constructed, others redirected. Some towns and villages too have changed almost beyond recognition over the past years. Some changes we expect, of course. Seasons change: this Spring the trees and flowers seem to have burst suddenly into leaf and blossom, all at once. Children grow up and become adults so soon. Not all change is bad. Some we even look forward to. The last year has been one of change for us: a new home, new job, a daughter married and we are soon to be grandparents. In this world of change, it's good to know of something - someone! - that never changes. And that is God. "The same yesterday, to-day and for ever" as the Bible puts it. His love for each one of us never changes. The offer of new life as we accept Jesus Christ as Saviour and Lord is still available to all who will receive it.

> **Lord, all my life I've been changing! I didn't choose; it simply happened.**
> **Thank you that as life goes on I realise that I myself can be more and more an instrument of change, in my own life, in the lives of those around me, and even in the society and world to which I belong.**
> **Let the sameness of Jesus yesterday, today and for ever be the basis of my being willing to change more and more into his likeness, through Jesus Christ Our Lord.**
> *Amen*

For further reading

Psalm 119:89-96   Enduring promises
Hebrews 13:5-8   The same yesterday, today and for ever

GOD'S FOOLISHNESS

For some reason I always seem to get the job of providing the message for April Fools' Day, and I've sometimes wondered why! But I take comfort from what the Bible says about being fools for Christ's sake. That is, being willing to be regarded by the world at large as a fool because we put Christ first and his service before personal ambition and even before personal comfort. And most certainly his glory before any of our own. Not of course that we don't get anything out of it! What price could you put on peace of mind and heart and a deep joy that stands with you when everything else may seem to be falling apart? That sort of peace comes only from a relationship with God which starts to develop when we accept Jesus Christ into our lives as Saviour and Lord. And do you know, God is a fool too. He is foolish enough to love us even when we are at our most unlovable and he is foolish enough to welcome us back when we have turned away from him in a self-seeking disobedience, and brought disaster on ourselves. How do I know? Because I've experienced that love and forgiveness myself and I have no hesitation in recommending to you the most wonderful discovery I have ever made. Will you be a fool for Christ's sake?

> Father I'm learning that what is wise and what is foolish
>   is all a matter of judgment.
> What some people think is wise others see to be folly.
> I remember that people thought the message of Jesus
>   dying on a cross was foolishness.
> But I know that through that foolishness the way of
>   lowly suffering love was established by which anyone
>   can be saved.
> So help me Lord to walk that foolish way, whatever the
>   world thinks, in order that I may play a little part in its
>   salvation, through Jesus Christ Our Lord.
>
> *Amen*

For further reading
1 Corinthians 1:18-25   Wiser than human wisdom
1 Corinthians 3:18-20   You must become a fool

TWO PICTURES OF GOD

I often think how lucky I am to do the job I do: I love words, and I enjoy meeting people, and I work as an interviewer! Jesus used words very simply when he met people. "Look at that farmer, sowing seed. Spreading the news about God is like that," he once said. He seemed to see pictures of God everywhere. Probably if we were looking out for them, we would too. I interviewed a photographer last week in a flat high above Holborn and found myself looking down on a street I knew well, but from a completely different viewpoint. Yesterday I was talking to a student in a comfy university common-room when suddenly there was a fire drill and we all hustled out with our books and papers into the pouring rain. One of those sudden April showers. "Wet clothes for the rest of the day!" I thought. But my student whipped out one of those fold up umbrellas from his jacket and we were companionable and dry till they let us in again. Two pictures of God! I am convinced that God does have an overall view, like the photographer. The first words in the Bible are: "In the beginning, God." But the way we meet him is more like my encounter with the student. In the thick of sorrows or joys we sense that he is with us, sharing our experience. Do you feel God is with you now? Are you glad about it? Or angry? Or what?

Oh God, I admit how easy it is to see only things in the
    shorter perspective.
Forgive me for concentrating almost entirely on the
    things nearest to me.
I thank you that life with you means seeing everything
    against the broadest possible backcloth of Creation
    through to the Redemption of everything.
That's the stage on which all of life is played out, I know.
Please help me to live with that broader perspective
    today and every day, through Jesus Christ Our Lord.

Amen

For further reading

Psalm 139:7-12   God everywhere
Acts 17:24-28   God very close to each one of us

LENT

PANCAKES AND SPRING CLEANING

In days gone by they were a means of using up eggs and other luxuries in the house on the eve of Lent. Nowadays, many of us continue this Shrove Tuesday tradition. Well, they taste so good! I'm talking of course about pancakes. Why is Lent on the Christian agenda? Well, it goes right back to the 4th century, when Christians began to set aside this forty day period running up to Easter. No doubt there's some link with Jesus' forty days of fasting in the wilderness. And Easter was also a time when many Christians were baptised, and these six weeks were an important part of their preparation. Lent has often been associated with giving up things. And that can be helpful if it leads us closer to Jesus. But it's certainly an opportunity to have a spiritual spring-clean! To get rid of any excess baggage in our lives that may be holding us back from following Jesus. Are there any things I need to put into the 'spiritual rubbish bin'? It takes time to work this out before God. And so, from now till Easter, it could be an opportunity to spend a little more time in listening to Jesus, as we read the Bible, and in speaking to him in prayer.

> **Lord, I know the need for a spiritual spring-clean in my life. I acknowledge those areas which have been cluttered with sin and failure.**
> **Even if my sins are great they are not too great for your mercy and kindness which is without limit.**
> **Forgive me and renew me in my love and service to Jesus Christ and give me strength to resist temptation and patience to endure.**
> **For the sake of Jesus Christ.**
>
> *Amen*

For further reading
Isaiah 58:3-11   Acceptable fasting
Matthew 6:16-18   Private fasting

HUMILITY AND SELF-IMPORTANCE

While I was thinking about what to say to-day a rather unusual sentence from the Bible came into my mind: "What does the Lord require of us, but to act justly, to love wholeheartedly and to walk humbly with our God." When did you last pray for humility? I can't remember when I did! Though God knows I need to. "Humility?" you may be thinking? "Isn't that a rather creepy, crawly Uriah Heepish sort of quality? No-one likes humble people." But is that true humility? I've been reading a book written by a nun, and she says that the thing that makes real humility so desirable is that it creates in us the possibility of a really close, intimate relationship with God. And what prevents this closeness, often, is that some of us are so stodged up with self-love and self-importance and self-indulgence that God cannot, so to speak, get through. And the fascinating thing about humility is that it clears away the obstacles between ourselves and God. It hollows out a sort of vacuum. And immediately that vacuum exists, God pours himself in. But we've got to want that badly enough, and pray for it with real longing. It helps too to remember that Christ set before us a picture of God's humility when he got down on his knees to wash the sweaty feet of his friends. I know that true humility is a quality I stand in need of. Perhaps the same is true of you.

> **Lord, why do I always have to be number one?**
> **Deliver me from the desire of wanting my**
> **own way with other people.**
> **Give me the heart for the towel and basin**
> **ministry, and help me to remember that when**
> **no one else was willing to wash feet, you did.**
> *Amen*

For further reading

Luke 18:9-14   Thank God I'm so much better than other people!
Romans 12:3-5   Don't think too highly of yourself

BEING 'A CHRIST'

This country of ours is still nominally a Christian country, and most people, if stopped in the street, would say they were 'Christian'. I've been doing a bit of Lent reading, and something I've found out is that in Germany a Christian is called 'Ein Christ'. Literally: a Christ. I find this rather daunting and challenging. It is so easy to shelter under our seemingly more general word of 'Christian' and live our lives as part-time followers, and half-hearted believers. But to be called 'a Christ' - now that is something, and surely not to be taken lightly or casually. Indeed, it could change our entire life. It isn't easy, I know, but perhaps one of the first steps could be to say and believe these words from the first letter of John: "If anyone acknowledges that Jesus is the Son of God, God lives in him and he in God." Then we can all say with St. Paul: "I have been crucified with Christ and I no longer live, but Christ lives in me."

> Lord Jesus help me to remember that as a
>   Christian, I bear your name in the world.
> Help me to be aware of your presence each day
>   so that I never squander a single moment of
>   my life.
> By your Spirit's power help me to be a Christian
>   who brings honour to the name of Christ.
> In Jesus' Name,
>
> *Amen.*

For further reading

Galatians 2:20-21   Christ lives in me
Philippians 3:7-11   All I want is to know Christ

DISTURBING BUT COMFORTING

I have never been one of those people who feel they must 'give up something for Lent.' Others do, I know, and find it helpful. But this I will say: there really isn't much point if it is done unwillingly, or because 'it's the thing to do.' When Samuel was choosing a new king for Israel, he followed God's 'methods': "I do not judge as man judges. Man looks at the outward appearance but I look at the heart." We cannot fool God. He knows our reasons for doing something. What a difference it would make to the way we live if we fully grasped that fact. As well as being rather disturbing, it can be very comforting too. Sometimes we do things for the best possible reasons only to be misunderstood by other people. But God says: "I do not judge as man judges. Man looks at the outward appearance but I look at the heart." Those are words we should consider very seriously as we approach Good Friday and Easter. Jesus suffered death on the cross to take the punishment for our sins. He did it willingly, because he loves us, and so that we might have a fresh start altogether. He is waiting for us not just to give up something for Lent but to give ourselves up to him. Then we shall find he will help us to live a life we won't be ashamed to let God see. And we can do this at any time - not just in Lent.

> You are the God to whom all hearts are open
> and from whom no secrets are hidden, and
> this day I trust myself to your grace which
> forgives and your power which enables.
> May I be swift to give up my selfish ambitions.
> Deliver me from the fear of always worrying
> what other people think and the foolishness
> of seeking to appear in a good light.
> Make me eager to take up the cross of self-
> denial so that I may be unashamed to confess
> you before a watching world.
> In Jesus' Name
>
> *Amen*

For further reading
Matthew 23:25-28   Jesus condemns hypocrisy
2 Corinthians 5:11-16   Pride in outward show

Hello! This is MESSAGE...

HOLY WEEK

AN INCREDIBLE FACT

I expect that at some time you have had something to do with small children. One thing's for sure: you always know exactly what they want and when they want it. They are quick to let everybody know about it They want and need their parents. Sometimes, and only sometimes, can they realise that their parents want and need them. As God's children, I think we probably behave rather like that: we spend a lot of time telling God of our wants and needs, but don't consider the question: "Does God need us?" At Easter time we read of the events of Holy Week. At the Last Supper on the Thursday, St. Luke tells us that Jesus said, "I have wanted so much to eat this Passover with you before I suffer." After supper they went into the garden of Gethsemane and Jesus wanted his disciples with him. And when he went to pray, he wanted Peter, James and John to be with him. Jesus wanted, and perhaps even needed, the company of his disciples, just as earlier in his ministry he wanted the little children to come to him and had been displeased with his disciples when they tried to stop them. So shall we now try to take in this incredible fact that it is not just we who want Jesus but it is also Jesus who actually wants us.

> Lord, you have made me reflect on all the
>   things you borrowed during your time on
>   earth.
> You were born in a borrowed stable.
> You preached from a borrowed boat.
> You rode into the city on a borrowed donkey.
> You broke bread in a borrowed upper room.
> You were buried in a borrowed tomb.
> You are the King of glory - and you need me.
> I joyfully surrender all that I am in the service
>   of such a King.
>
> *Amen*

For further reading

Mark 10:13-16   Let the children come to me
Luke 22:14-20   I have longed to share this final meal with you

SO MUCH TO LEARN

The scene in the upper room just before the Last Supper must have been a rather disturbing one. Everyone was worried. Rumours of impending doom were circulating. People were anxious, sad and harassed. Only Jesus was calm, though it was to Jesus that all these disturbing things were threatening to happen. Yet it was Jesus who remembered the custom of the day, and he took a towel and bowl and began to wash the feet of his disciples. Perhaps the clue to the mystery is in the phrase: "Jesus, knowing that he came from the father and was going to the father...took a towel etc." Sure of his divine origin, and sure of his divine destiny, the one who was about to be crucified could still be calm. It is truly an amazing story. There is so much that we can learn from it. In the midst of the great storms and disturbances of life, we can have a safe and sure anchor in Christ. We too can be sure of our divine origin and divine destiny if we put our faith in Jesus. We too can know a deep inner serenity whatever is going on around us. I think we can also learn from this story that no task is too menial for us to do for one another. He who came amongst us to serve calls us also into service, and in this we can find true satisfaction and fulfilment.

> Lord, in the hour of your greatest need you gave
>   us your greatest gifts.
> In the garden of Gethsamene you gave up your
>   will to the Father's purpose.
> In the upper room you gave us a meal to
>   remember.
> On the cross of Calvary you gave us your life
>   and shed your blood.
> And now I ask a further gift.
> Please give me in the moments of my greatest
>   need the same sense of strong purpose which
>   ruled your life.
> In your Name,
>
> *Amen*

For further reading

John 13:12-17   Do you understand what I have done for you?
Philippians 2:5-11   He assumed the nature of a slave

THE UPSIDE-DOWN KINGDOM

Have you ever waited patiently in a queue when someone pushes in front of you? Personally, I find that makes me furious. In some countries they don't seem to bother to queue at all. It's just each man for himself in one pushing, heaving mass, which is even worse. It seems to reflect a rather unpleasant, selfish side of human nature. I see it every day on the roads as I drive into London, people trying to push in from side roads and others not letting them in. Or on motorways when three lanes are merging into two for some roadworks or other. Some drivers stay in the third lane till the last possible minute and then force their way in, in front of everyone else, don't they? It's the me-first mentality. One of the amazing things that Jesus teaches us is that God, who created the universe and has the right to be first in every queue, isn't like that. He teaches us that in his Kingdom those who try to push to the front will be last, while those who waited patiently at the back will be first. Before his last supper with his friends, he himself took on the role of a servant. This is part of the upside-down nature of the Kingdom, where love, for all its apparent weakness and vulnerability, turns out to be the only force strong enough to overcome evil. And perhaps the most amazing thing of all is that God himself loves us despite all our faults, and has invited us into his Kingdom. It's an invitation we'd be daft to refuse.

> **Lord, I like to think I am too sophisticated to be
> a queue jumper, but I know in my heart that
> there are too many times when I love to be
> first.**
> **Help me to grow in the life-style of the
> Kingdom where the first shall be last and the
> meek are blessed, and those who go on and
> on forgiving know the fullness of joy.**
> **In your Name,**
>
> *Amen*

For further reading

Mark 9:33-35   Arguments about status
Luke 14:7-11   Jockeying for position

GOD IS LIKE CHRIST

Haven't you sometimes said: "How can one know what God is like? He is so great and sometimes seems so far away." Recently I came across a sentence from one of to-day's Christian writers and it throws real light on the problem. It reads like this: "The heart of Christian doctrine is not only that Jesus is divine, but that God is Christlike." Now, if God's like Christ, that's wonderful. I can read about him. I can see him shining in Christ's actions and love and patience and forgiveness. Jesus says he came to show us the father. So we are in fact allowed to know something about him. He told his followers, during the last week of his life, "Whoever has seen me has seen the father. The words that I have spoken to you do not come from me. The father, who remains in me, does his own work." Many of us acknowledge that Jesus is divine, that by his life and death and resurrection he has brought deliverance to each one who will accept it from him. But add to that the knowledge that God is like Christ, and that we may see him in seeing Christ: this is a great revelation! It makes us rich indeed.

> O Lord God Eternal, greater in majesty than I
>   can ever imagine, stronger than any power I
>   can comprehend, thank you that your son,
>   Jesus, has opened my eyes not only to your
>   greatness but also to your nearness.
> Thank you that you are closer to me than I can
>   even believe.
> You are fully aware of my needs even when I
>   can't express them in words.
> You are truly a friend in high places.
>
> *Amen*

For further reading

John 14:6-14 Whoever has seen me has seen the Father
2 Corinthians 4:5-6 God's glory shining in the face of Christ

OUR ACCENTS GIVE US AWAY

My mother was born in Sheffield. She left there when she was thirteen, and for the past forty years has been living in Hove. But she still speaks with a Yorkshire accent. Yes, our accents give us away. That was what happened to Peter, one of the disciples of Jesus. When Jesus was arrested in the garden of Gethsemane and taken away for questioning, Peter, like all the others, was frightened. Nevertheless he decided to follow at a safe distance and even made his way into the courtyard of the High Priest's house, where Jesus had been taken. There was a fire in the courtyard and people crowded round it for warmth. Peter moved nearer and joined them, no doubt trying to remain inconspicuous and unrecognised, but he was forced to speak: "You're one of them! Your accent betrays you!" he was accused. As followers of Jesus to-day, we should be marked out by our accent. It's recognised in the sorts of things we say and do. It's an accent of caring. It's loving concern for other people and their troubles and worries. It's help that's given freely, gladly and without stint. Jesus said, "Whatever you do for other people, you are doing for me."

> Lord, I thank you for my human accent which reminds
>   me of my physical roots.
> Forgive me when I am ashamed of my background.
> Thank you for my upbringing. Thank you for those who
>   first taught me about your love. I especially name .....
> Lord, I thank you for my Christ-like accent which
>   reminds me of my spiritual roots in you.
> Forgive me when I have tried to disguise the way I
>   speak.
> May this accent grow stronger each day.
> Let your Spirit inspire my mind, let your wisdom shape
>   my words, let your love control my body that my
>   whole being may glorify you.
>
> *Amen*

For further reading

Matthew 26:69-75   Peter's denial
Colossians 3:12-17   The things we say and do

AMAZING LOVE

What IS the great message of Holy Week? It is this: that God is Love. That is at the heart of what the Christian talks about. And the reason he goes on and on talking about the wonder of the love of God is because of the tremendous 'giving' that God gave of himself for us on the cross on the first Good Friday. But it isn't just that God is love. It is, to use the words of St. Paul, that "God was in Christ, reconciling the world to himself". What lies behind that expression is so utterly wonderful that you can understand why one of the great Good Friday hymns puts it this way: " Were the whole realm of Nature mine, that were an offering far too small. Love so amazing, so divine, demands my soul, my life, my all." How about changing that word 'demand' into 'shall have.'

> **When I survey the wondrous cross on which the**
> **Prince of glory died -**
> **I see forgiveness - please make me clean.**
> **I see love - please give me compassion.**
> **I see light - please renew my vision.**
> **I see life - please help me to live for you now**
> **and forever**
>
> *Amen*

For further reading

2 Corinthians 5:18-21   The message of reconciliation
1 John 4:7-16   God is love

Hello! This is MESSAGE...

GOOD FRIDAY:
THE CROSS

A GOD WHO SUFFERS

It's a great pity that in the hustle and bustle of modern life few seem to spend time thinking about the real meaning of Easter. For me, Easter is the most moving time in the Christian calendar, because it reminds me that our God is not a far-away king lording it over his subjects from a golden palace, but someone close who cares so much for each one of us, yes, even you and me, that he would make any sacrifice for us. A God who suffers for us. I know the problem of pain and suffering is not an easy one to understand, and nor is the mystery of God's love for me, but when I'm suffering and tempted to ask, "Why is this happening to me?" I take comfort from knowing that God, the creator and ruler of the universe, can understand and share my suffering, for he has suffered far more than I ever will. He sent his only son to die, to save us. My thoughts are summed up in the words of a well-known hymn:

> "And when I think that God, his son not sparing,
> Sent him to die - I scarce can take it in
> That on the cross my burden gladly bearing
> He bled and died to take away my sin.
> Then sings my soul, my saviour God to thee,
> How great thou art, how great thou art."

> **Lord, out of eternity you focused your love for**
> **us in an unforgettable moment in time.**
> **From space your love for us was anchored in**
> **wood and earth, in nails and crown of thorns.**
> **In Jesus you lifted the cloud of unknowing to**
> **give us a glimpse into your Universe of glory.**
> **To this Prince of Glory, lifted up, we are**
> **inexorably drawn as he gives us a strange**
> **strength to endure our own suffering,**
> **knowing that he understands, heals our pain**
> **by his stripes and lifts us up into oneness**
> **with him.**

For further reading

Psalm 22:1-5   My God, why hast thou forsaken me?
Hebrews 2:9   The test of suffering

IS IT NOTHING TO YOU?

For the past few years Good Friday seems to have become just an ordinary day. The shops open as normal, and no-one seems to realise what Good Friday is all about. I think this must grieve the Lord Jesus very much, because this is a very important day in the life of any Christian. The day that Jesus died a cruel death for the sake of each one of us. I wonder why people have started to be so indifferent to Good Friday? Perhaps they don't really believe these things about Jesus. Perhaps they just don't care. If you get the chance this Easter time, listen to Stainer's 'Crucifixion'. The music and singing are beautiful, but try also to listen to the words. The part which says, "God so loved the world that he gave his only begotten son that who so believeth in him should not perish but have everlasting life." Then again, the part which says, "Is it nothing to you, all ye who pass by?" These words never fail to move me. If you have never given much thought to all these things please think about them now, this Good Friday, and then rejoice with the rest of us on Easter Sunday, knowing that Jesus rose from the dead and is alive to-day. I'll leave you with this question: "Is it nothing to you?"

> Make us aware and sensitive, O Lord, to all that is
>   happening in the world around us; the humble battles
>   that are being won; the integrity which is being
>   preserved against all odds; the faith that is being
>   poured into life each day.
> In myriad ways the world is being redeemed by ordinary
>   people.
> Make us sensitive to the sacrifice that is being made by
>   others that enables us to enjoy so much that we take
>   for granted.
> May each day become a sacrament to us and in its
>   pattern may we see the outline of a Cross which is
>   woven into the very fabric of creation.

For further reading

Lamentations 1:12   No-one cares about my pain
Galatians 6:14   God forbid that I should boast of anything but the Cross

PAIN AND REJECTION

I have been reflecting on how it must have felt to be one of the disciples of Jesus in those last days leading up to the events of what we now call Good Friday. I should imagine they were somewhat confused but probably excited. Jesus was obviously preparing them for something special, the culmination of his ministry on earth, but they had little idea what was ahead. They must have had that feeling of excited anticipation we witness in our children as their birthday or Christmas approaches. If they had known what was ahead, the disciples would have seen the cross as total failure and humiliation. I remember the disappointment and feeling of failure when I kept rolling backwards down the steepest hill I had encountered in London during my first driving test, realising my chances of passing had slipped away. But that experience made my feeling of joy even greater a few months later when I passed. Having suffered the despair of bereavement, the exhilaration of witnessing the new life as my daughter was born was heightened. The cross is not an entirely negative symbol, because it depicts Christ's love and sacrifice for us, taking upon himself our sin. However, it undoubtedly represented pain and rejection. But without the agony, we could not have the ecstasy of the resurrection, which brings the certain knowledge of the living Lord who loves each one of us.

> One of your greatest gifts to us, O Father, is hope - the
> eager looking forward to new and better things.
> We thank you for our dreams of a new world and a new
> life, but sometimes they are not your dreams and do
> not belong to your Kingdom.
> Help us to see your purpose in plans which go astray, in
> hopes which are dashed, and may we find the bed
> rock of joy on the other side of defeat and despair, the
> ecstasy through the agony, the light beyond the
> darkness and so learn the secret of Our Lord's
> strength and inward peace.

For further reading

Mark 10:32-40   Jesus began to tell them what would happen
John 13:1-11   He knew that his hour had come

WE'RE WRONG

I don't know about you, but more and more as I listen to the news, I've come to the conclusion that much of the trouble in the world is caused by people who are certain that they are right and others are wrong. Their way is the only way, their beliefs are the only correct ones, their view of life, their politics, their ambitions, even their culture are the only ones worth having. It's not a bad thing to remember that the first step in becoming a Christian is to realise that we are wrong, which is one of the things I find very attractive and unusual. We have to face the fact that we do and say the wrong things and fail to do and say the right things. In other words we need help. We need God. We're not perfect. We're wrong. Jesus didn't die on the cross for people who know they're right. He died for people who realise they've made a mess of many things. That's when we can turn to God. And the good news that sometimes gets lost in a lot of talk is that we are loved, accepted and forgiven by God and can get going again with new strength from him. He doesn't leave us grovelling pathetically at his feet. He says, "Get up. Go! Love and serve your neighbour."

> Lord teach us humility and make us open to all
>   that you have to teach us.
> Lord make us teachable; refine our faith and
>   renew our minds that they may not be
>   imprisoned in blind dogmas but released into
>   the wonder of each experience and the
>   knowledge that you are still making your
>   world and your people in your own image.

For further reading

Isaiah 53:4-7   The Lord laid on him the guilt of us all
Romans 5:6-11   Christ died for the wicked

GOLGOTHA

When I visited Israel, it was a strange experience to see on a passing bus the name of its destination: 'Golgotha'. The only other time I had heard of the place was in the accounts of Jesus' crucifixion. I found it hard to realise that such a place still existed. This set my imagination to work, and I saw in my mind's eye the scramble at the bus station when the conductor shouted, "Golgotha! All change!" Then my thoughts turned back almost 2,000 years, to the time of the crucifixion. That really was the time of 'All change!' For the Lord Jesus opened up a new way of life for us when he was crucified there. He suffered for you and me. All mankind was on the wrong road but the Lord Jesus opened the way to everlasting life. A complete change of direction. "I am the way," he said, "I am Truth and I am Life." We can turn to him and talk to him as we would to a trusted friend. Each age has its special problems, but however small or large we can bring them to the cross. "Come to me, all you who have burdens," he said, "and I will give you rest." We shall never have true joy and peace until we make that 'all change' and ask the Lord Jesus to take control.

> In life's pilgrimage, O God, you bring us to the
> hilltop where great vistas open before us; to
> points of no return; to places which seem to
> be dead ends.
> Each part of our journey can change us if we let
> it. Help us to follow Jesus in imagination on
> his journey and see even in our darkest hour
> of trial and anguish the shining of the eternal
> light.

For further reading

Mark 15:22-39   They crucified him

Hebrews 10:19-23   He opened for us a new, living way

I CRUCIFIED THE SON OF GOD

Perhaps you have heard about Rembrandt's famous painting of 'The Three Crosses'. In the centre is the cross on which Jesus died, with the crowd at the foot of the cross. The different facial expressions and actions of the people involved in the awful crime of crucifying the Son of God are shown. At the edge of the painting is another figure, almost hidden in the shadows. Art critics say this is a representation of Rembrandt himself, for he recognised that by his sins he had helped to nail Jesus to the cross. We find it easy to blame the Roman soldiers or Pontius Pilate for Christ's death. It is quite a simple thing to say that Jesus died for the sins of the world, but it is quite another thing to say that Jesus died for my sins. It was I who nailed him to the cross. I crucified the Son of God. I joined the mockery. Like the one who was almost hidden in the crowd in the painting, we too are standing there with Rembrandt. But then recall what Jesus said as he hung on the cross, "Father, forgive them." Thank God that includes you and me.

> We cannot detach ourselves, O Lord, from the
> world or remain aloof from its pain and sin.
> We are part of the world and each action and
> decision we make flows into the mainstream
> of its life.
> We contribute to suffering as well as to
> salvation; we heal and hurt by our words and
> deeds.
> Forgive us our sins and from a changed and
> redeemed life may we witness to the power
> and love of the Christ who died for us all on
> the Cross.

For further reading

Matthew 26:26-28   This is my body, this is my blood
Luke 23:32-34   Father, forgive them for they know not what they do

THE MYSTERIOUS KEY

I'm just a local housewife you're listening to to-day. Occasionally we get a lord or a bishop to record the week's messages. But not this week! I've been wondering what St. Paul would talk to you about if he only had two minutes. (We know he once preached so long that a young man lost consciousness and fell out of a window. But that's another story.) I do know exactly what St. Paul would say, because he once wrote about it in a letter. This is what he said: "I preach Christ crucified, a message that is offensive to some and nonsense to others, but to those who understand it, it is the very key to the meaning of life." But you know, even to the most long-standing Christian, the cross is still full of mystery. God dying for us! Here's a story I found helpful: it is recorded that on one occasion a judge found himself obliged to pass sentence on a prisoner whom he recognised as a boyhood friend. Naturally, he would willingly have let the man go free. But justice compelled him to administer the law. So when the man was found 'guilty' the judge sentenced him to pay the heaviest penalty possible. But then he laid aside his judicial robes and stepped down beside the prisoner... and paid the penalty himself.

> We acknowledge that you are a holy God, that
> you have placed holiness and righteousness
> at the centre of your world.
> When we ignore your laws of life we not only
> reject your love but stand condemned and in
> need of help.
> Lord you love us even when we have sinned.
> Your Son's death at Calvary takes away the
> sin of the world and our sin.
> Lord have mercy upon us.
> Strengthen all those who uphold your
> righteousness and who themselves pay the
> price of the folly of those they love.

For further reading

1 Corinthians 2:1-5   Christ, nailed to the cross
1 Peter 1:17-21   The blood of Christ

THE FINAL SACRIFICE

It so happens that because of the job I do, many people over many years have come to me in confidence and poured out their deepest fears and anxieties. So I know at first hand that one of the problems that human beings experience is the problem of guilt. It affects our relationships with other people. It warps our attitude to society. It spoils the regard in which we are able to hold ourselves. How can there be hope for deliverance from guilt feelings? The point of the death of Jesus was that his was the sacrifice as the Lamb of God to make forgiveness a reality. Such an expression takes a bit of understanding, but we have to remember the Jewish background of Jesus. Sacrifices brought the chance of forgiveness, and Jesus' sacrifice was the final act that made all other sacrifices unnecessary. When Christ rose from the grave, the world could understand that the sacrifice of his life was not a heroic failure. It brought the word 'forgiveness' within the grasp of human experience. And the starting point of that is the death and resurrection of the Son of God.

> "O Lord, you have searched me and you know me. You
>   know when I sit and when I rise; you perceive my
>   thought from afar, you discern my going out and my
>   lying down; you are familiar with all my ways."
> You know our fears, you know our guilty feelings, O
>   Lord. Often the hardest thing of all is to forgive
>   ourselves and forgiving others does not come easily to
>   us.
> Yet you have opened a door into freedom for us.
> From the Cross we hear the amazing words, "Father
>   forgive them..." and in your risen power we hear your
>   words, "It is I, do not be afraid..."
> Help us to trust these words of forgiveness and
>   assurance and live in the freedom of your victory over
>   all that imprisons us.

For further reading

Psalm 51:1-5   The burden of guilt
Hebrews 10:11-18   Sins forgiven and forgotten

THE CROSS: A STRANGE LOGO

Have you ever thought what a strange logo the Christian religion has? I suppose most religions have a sign, a sort of trademark. There's the hammer and sickle of communism, the half-moon of the Moslems. But I think the most extraordinary one by far is the Christian one: not a throne, to show that God is a ruler, nor a world, to show he's a creator, but - how would anyone believe it? - a cross. Two pieces of wood to which men took their God when he came to visit and love them. And they hanged him by his hands and feet till he was dead. On the cross. Yet out of this worst possible evil God brought the greatest triumph. Love took on evil, our evil, and conquered it. Came through as victor! He called out from the cross: "It is accomplished!" From the cross he stretched out, as it were, one hand to man and the other to God and linked us up. We come to God 'through Jesus Christ our Lord' as many prayers say, and the cross, the way of suffering made it possible. It's no wonder that Christians reverence the cross and are so very grateful for it. Our strange sign - the sign that love has won the victory for us.

> **In your Cross O Jesus, your humanity and your godhead meet.**
> **At the intersection of wood bisecting heaven and earth we find the confluence of hatred and love, sin and salvation, selfishness and sacrifice.**
> **Your outstretched arms embrace the world, your pain-racked body absorbs all its cruelty and blindness.**
> **The instrument of your death has become our sign of victory.**
> **May we never cheapen it or turn away from its piercing and so may its healing flow into our lives and into our world...**

For further reading

Matthew 21:33-46   The main cornerstone
John 19:16-18, 28-30   The victory accomplished

LOVING HANDS

As my friend left this morning, I noticed a small badge on the lapel of her coat. It was a tiny replica of Durer's painting, 'The Praying Hands'. Hands - what a great deal they tell us about people. A pianist's hands differ from a gardener's, yet both create something beautiful. The new born baby's hands are small and delicate; an old person's hands tell a story of work and of age. When Jesus was on earth, he used his hands to help others. His were strong hands for he was a carpenter. They were gentle, loving hands too, reaching out to help, to heal, to comfort, to encourage. He laid his hands on many: the leper, the sick, the outcast. He gathered children in his arms and held out his hands in friendship to those others didn't want to know. The night of his betrayal, he took on the task of the humblest servant, washing the feet of his disciples. In the end those hands were nailed to a cross and he was hoisted up to die a painful death. After his resurrection, Jesus came to his friends and showed them his nailed hands, blessed them and assured them of the reality of eternal life. Now he has no hands on earth to do his work but ours.

Held in your hands O Father, we pass our days.
Your guardian power protects us yet we are not
    cocooned against evil and adversity: our
    freedom in the world you have made allows
    us to hurt and to be hurt, to grow by
    mistakes.
The nails that held your Son on the Cross reveal
    the chosen helplessness by which you hand
    your task over to us.
You entrust your Kingdom into our frail hands.
You hold us and in that holding we hold you,
    and so the whole world is in your hands.

For further reading

Mark 1:40-42   Jesus heals a leper
1 Corinthians 12:12-27   Now you are Christ's body

Hello! This is MESSAGE...

EASTER SUNDAY: THE RESURRECTION

VICTORY OVER DEATH

Easter is a season of joy. Let me say why. People throughout history have been worried about death. It looms in front of everyone, and while we don't like talking about it, we know it is inevitable. Here comes Jesus. He dies, and his death is a particularly horrible one. He is buried. Then he is seen alive in a garden. And the implication of that is that death is not the end. God who sent his son to be the saviour of the world has broken the power of death and shown that there is life beyond the grave. St. Paul uses a rather strange expression: "The first fruits of them that sleep." He means by that that Christ's coming to life again, his resurrection, is the first sign of new life. Others who believe in Christ can expect likewise to rise to new life because of him. That's what makes joy so wonderful an Easter word. The power of death to frighten and to cause despair no longer need dominate. Christ's victory over death is for sharing with us.

So much of my life is death.
The dead time when nothing is happening.
The slow death of relationships turning sour.
The dead child within me, who was me.
The deadening of memory, sensitivity, love.
Call me out of this tomb, Lord.
Let me live in you.

For further reading

John 20:11-18   Seen alive in a garden
1 Corinthians 15:12-22   The fact is: Christ was raised from death

CHRIST IS RISEN!

Looking through some of the Easter cards on sale in shops, I have the impression that for many people Easter is a vague rejoicing that Springtime has come round again. Easter is believed to be nothing more than a Spring holiday, heralding the Spring flowers, blossoming trees, and, we hope, warmer days. To the Christian, Easter means much more than this. The beauty of Springtime, with its abundance of new life reminds us of the life that was released on the first Easter Day. Our Easter faith is a resurrection faith, a trust in Christ who was raised from death and who is now and always our risen and living Lord. For the Christian, each day is a celebration of our Lord's triumphant victory of life over death and love over hate. Every day we live in his risen presence and walk in his company. "Jesus lives! Christ is risen!" is as true to-day as it was on the first Easter morning. I found a poem which ends with these words: "This is the resurrecting power, through every age the same." This is the truth about Easter: Our Lord is risen. Thanks be to God.

> Send a little Springtime
> To the Winter of my unbelief.
> Let the rays of your loving kindness,
> Release me from the cold, damp earth of death
> Drawn into the radiance of your eternal brightness.

For further reading

Luke 24:1-12   Why search among the dead for one who lives?
Colossians 3:1-4   You have been raised to life with Christ

61

RESURRECTION FAITH

I expect like me you sometimes get a bit impatient with politicians being interviewed on TV when they don't seem able to give a straight answer to a straight question. They won't call a spade a spade. St. Paul was just the opposite, and Easter time always reminds me of a very blunt remark he once made: "If Jesus Christ didn't rise from the dead, our Christian faith is empty, worthless and hopeless." And that's fair comment. No-one can prove the resurrection. But when you look at how his followers reacted to seeing him alive again, back from the grave, they were all shaken to the core, even afraid. Scarcely able to believe their own eyes. Even they had been convinced that death had finally taken Jesus from them. All this rings very true all these centuries later. If Peter and John and the rest had planned to cook up a story about Jesus being alive again, they'd have said to all the doubters: "We told you so, didn't we! This is what we knew would happen and it has!" But in fact they were as amazed as everyone else. And that thought has helped me to confirm my faith this Easter. So I pass it on to you.

> Don't look me in the eye, Lord
>   and ask me to believe.
> Don't pry into my actions,
>   or the motives of my heart.
> Don't shine on me the harsh light
>   of your righteousness.
> But wait for me, like waiting for a friend
> Still searching for something important.

For further reading

Luke 24:36-44   They thought they were seeing a ghost
1 Peter 1:3-6   Resurrection hope

HOPE BEYOND HOPE

I wonder if you've ever dreamt of having the chance to make a totally fresh start, to find your life full of new beginnings, new opportunities, new experiences. Like a driver who gets rid of an old car with lots wrong with it and owns a new car that is fast, reliable and impressive. Or like an invalid who suddenly finds his disease is being cured. Or like a businessman going bankrupt who finds one day that overnight everyone wants his product. To-day is Easter, the day of resurrection, the day when Jesus, who was dead, shares his new life with all the world. To-day is the day of new beginnings and hope beyond hope. A dead man coming back to life would be remarkable, a strange event from long ago. But a God who has lived, died, and now lives eternally is something different, for two reasons: first of all, this new life is offered to us all as a hope for life after death for ourselves and for those we love. And secondly, it is offered to us now as a new way of living, a new power in our lives, a new friendship with God himself. You find everything changed on Easter Day. It is the day when life comes out of death, hope out of despair, light out of darkness. For Jesus lives. And he can live in you.

Dare I hope, God, that you hear me now?
That you care for me,
I, who don't really care for myself?

For further reading

John 16:16-22 No-one will rob you of your joy
Romans 6:1-14   We believe we will live, with him

WE SHALL SEE HIM

Seeing is not necessarily believing. Nor is hearing for that matter. This is clear from the stories about Jesus after the resurrection. Mary Magdalene just could not believe her eyes when she saw Jesus in the garden after his resurrection. Nor could she believe her ears. It was only when Jesus said "Mary," that she knew she was both seeing and hearing her Lord. The two disciples going to Emmaus did not believe their eyes or ears when Jesus joined and walked with them. It was only when he broke bread for them that they realised who he was. When the disciples went fishing on the Sea of Galilee and Jesus called to them from the shore, they didn't recognise him at first. But after obeying his command, they made a huge catch of fish and then knew it really was Jesus. What does all this tell us? Surely that, although we cannot see Jesus with our human eyes nor hear him with our human ears yet we can still find him. We shall see him in the simple everyday things of life like the sharing of a meal. We shall see him in some miracle like a crowd of people responding to the preaching of the gospel. Above all perhaps we shall meet Jesus in those peaceful moments when we are alone and quiet and we hear him call us by name in the depths of our soul. He came that we might have life, life in all its fullness.

Come to me.
[pray in silence]
Jesus.
[pray in silence]
Jesus, come to me.
[pray in silence]
Come, quickly.

For further reading

Luke 24:13-35   The road to Emmaus
John 21:1-14   The sea of Tiberias

DOUBTING THOMAS

There's one character in the Bible who didn't enjoy Easter. His name was Thomas. And when he heard the story of the resurrection of Jesus he found it so impossible he couldn't believe it. A week later, however, everything changed for Thomas. He met with the risen Christ and was invited actually to put his hands into the side of Jesus. The impossible had become the actual. Doubting Thomas became believing Thomas. People often find it hard to believe the Easter story. After all, dead people don't spring back to life in the everyday world of human experience. It seems so impossible. But once we can experience the living Jesus, doubt turns to faith. There's a chorus that puts it like this: "You ask me how I know he lives? He lives within my heart." I reckon Thomas's belated Easter was a day he was never to forget. His outburst, "My Lord and my God!" was as full-blooded a devotion to Jesus as anyone could offer. How about following in Thomas's steps to-day.

It was easy for Thomas
You came back to see him:
    he saw you and believed.
Fill me with your presence.
So I, too, may know that
    you are my Lord, and my God.

For further reading

John 20:19-29   Thomas said, "My Lord and my God!"
Acts 26:1-32   Paul describes his encounter with the risen Christ

65

I SEND YOU

I suppose it would be easy to think of Easter as a time simply to stand back in amazement. Speechless. Transfixed to the spot. Awestruck. If we're not like that we've missed the point. But then what? I've been looking again at the very first time Jesus appeared to the disciples as a group on the evening of the very first Easter Day. He said to them, "Peace." Then they heard this challenge, "As my father has sent me, even so send I you." From then on the task of Christians has been plain and straightforward. Jesus came to show us what God is like. He cared, he loved, he gave, he understood, he transformed. That's what 'So send I you' means in to-day's world. The Christian is to care, to love, to give, to understand and to proclaim how people and how societies can be transformed. This really is the most wonderful collection of words and ideas. It makes the job of the Christian so clear. It means that the world does not have to struggle uncertainly from one crisis to another. Christ gives us hope. Christ gives hope to the church. Christ gives hope to the world. What a marvellous, marvellous day is Easter!

> Send me the deep peace, Lord
>   of doing your will.
> And if I don't quite make it,
> Love me anyway.
> I try in your name.

For further reading

Acts 1:6-11   Witnesses to the ends of the earth
2 Thessalonians 2:15-17   Encouragement to stand firm

THE ASCENSION

A PUZZLING EVENT

We are coming up to the day that appears in our diaries as Ascension Day. The year is rushing by all too fast, isn't it! You will recall the account in the first chapter of Acts, of Jesus finally leaving his friends and going up into heaven. I think we may find this event somewhat puzzling. But at the time his friends were obviously not bewildered by it. They were not left feeling bereft but, rather, full of joy. They were certain he was still with them in the way we sometimes feel the closeness of one we love, even in their absence. And they must have gone on being certain, for take a look at how they obeyed his command to "go into all the world and preach the gospel." This is the amazing fact, isn't it, that all down the ages, men and women who have been convinced of the living presence of Jesus in their lives have gone on spreading the good news and witnessing to the love of God. MESSAGE is a tiny part of this witness. So is your care for your neighbour, the time you give to voluntary work, your selflessness in the face of another's need, your sympathetic ear, your prayers for the suffering in the world. It is wonderful to be part of such a great cloud of witnesses, isn't it!

> Lord, help me not to feel lonely
>   in my witness for you this day.
> I am one among 'a great cloud of witnesses'.
> Make me bold, make me wise
>   and keep me faithful as I tell others
>   of your love and power.
>
> *Amen.*

For further reading

Acts 10:34-43   Peter preaches the gospel
Hebrews 12:1-3   The great cloud of witnesses

GREAT JOY

Seeing people off isn't usually a happy task. Perhaps it is at a railway station and we wave until they are out of sight and then make our lonely way back along the platform and back home. Or perhaps we wave their car off until it is out of sight, and then go back into the house and wonder when we will see them again. It is especially difficult if it is someone very close to us and we know how much we will miss them. On Ascension Day we think of Jesus departing from his disciples. Right at the end of Luke's gospel we read just one or two sentences about this event. Yet, though short, they are really quite extraordinary. Here they are: "Jesus led them out as far as Bethany. Then, with arms outstretched, he departed from them. And they returned with great joy and were continually in the temple praising God." Jesus, their great friend and saviour was going out of their presence...and yet they returned with great joy. The secret is of course that he was leading them to know a new kind of presence. As Dr. Maltby put it in his book, 'The Meaning of the Resurrection', "he took his physical presence away from some men to give his spiritual presence to all men...he went out of some men's sight into all men's hearts." For a long time the disciples had been learning from Jesus what this would mean. "Abide with me," he said, "and I in you." Or again, "Lo, I am with you always, even to the end of the world." So they could return with joy for they were daring to claim all his promises as true for themselves. Nothing now, ever, any more, could separate them from their living Lord. And all this is true for us too as we believe his promises.

> Lord, knowing that your resurrection and
> ascension have released you into all the
> world, I claim the sense of your presence
> with me just now.
> Help me to believe that,
> as I face the challenges in my life,
> I am never alone.
> You are with me.
>
> *Amen.*

For further reading

Luke 24:45-53   The ascension story
Romans 8:31-39   No more separation - ever!

I AM WITH YOU ALWAYS

A young Chinese Christian, named Lo, was given a new Testament to read. When he found in Matthew's gospel the words "Lo, I am with you always," he was greatly excited because he took this as a personal promise Although he misinterpreted the first word of that text for his own name, Lo didn't miss the impact of the verse. We too may read our own name into the promise. "Sue, Geoffrey, Chris, Dorothy...I am with you always." Jesus gave these reassuring words to his disciples because he knew how lonely they would feel when he departed from them and the full burden of the task of spreading the good news became theirs. He would not be with them physically. They would no longer see his look or encouragement or hear his voice in the sane way. Knowing the weakness of human nature, he consoled then with the promise that he would still be with them in the person of the Holy Spirit, and he would assist them in preaching, teaching, living and witnessing. Whatever your name is, you can be sure that Jesus is just as much with you as he is with Lo.

> Lord, there are hurdles I have to overcome
>   this day.
> There may be unexpected obstacles on my path.
> Give me the confidence that knows you are
>   with me to help me,
>   to strengthen me and to give me direction.
> *Amen.*

For further reading

Joshua 1:9   I am with you, wherever you go
Isaiah 43:1-5   You are precious to me

PENTECOST:
THE HOLY SPIRIT

GOD'S POWER

It's when there's a power cut that we realise how much we depend on electricity. The lights, fridge, TV, washing machine, heaters, all become useless. It may also mean we can't boil a kettle or cook a meal. What a relief when power is restored. Electricity is a great power, an essential of modern life. One wonders how earlier generations managed without it. On the anniversary of Pentecost, we remember the day when God's power filled the first disciples and the Christian church was born. The book of Acts, chapter 2, tells the dramatic story: "When the day of Pentecost came, all the believers were gathered together in one place. Suddenly, there was a noise from the sky which sounded like a strong wind blowing, and it filled the whole house where they were sitting. Then they saw what looked like tongues of fire which spread out and touched each person there. They were all filled with the Holy Spirit." We cannot understand how God's power works in human life but we can see the effect. Where God's spirit lives in a Christian, certain things happen. There is courage for living, strength to do things that would otherwise seem impossible. God's spirit helps people to give and forgive, to love and serve. And there are no power cuts with God's spirit. If we are linked to God in prayer, his power will flow into our life and we shall be truly alive for him.

> **Father in heaven,**
> **may your Holy Spirit, so powerful and free,**
> **renew my mind and heart in love for Jesus**
> **and for my sisters and brothers.**
> **May there be peace among us,**
> **to the glory of your name.**
>
> *Amen.*

For further reading

Acts 4:13-20   Ordinary men doing extraordinary things
2 Timothy 1:7-10   The Spirit gives us power

HOLY SPIRITED PEOPLE

If you asked people in the street what 'Whitsun' or 'Pentecost' meant, I wonder how many would be able to tell you? It's funny how most people know about the meaning of Christmas and have got some idea of the significance of Good Friday but know far less about this festival. Yet it's so important to the Christian faith. The followers of Jesus, the same ones who deserted him and left him to face death alone, are now filled with astonishing faith and courage. Nothing will prevent them from telling the world of the wonderful truth they have discovered. They are put into prison and flogged, and even put to death, but nothing stops them. So what was it that changed their lives so dramatically? Or rather who? The Bible tells us that it was the Holy Spirit on that first Whit Sunday who 'filled' them as Jesus had promised, giving them power to speak out boldly and fearlessly. I could do with some of that courage too, couldn't you? That same promise is ours to-day, so we needn't be timid. We can ask God's Holy Spirit to change our lives as he changed the first disciples. The world could do with a lot more holy spirited people right now.

Father, send forth your Spirit upon us that,
    like the first Christians, we might witness to
    the resurrection of your Son, Jesus Christ,
    with courage and enthusiasm.
Keep us joyful in your service.
This we ask through Christ our Lord.

Amen.

For further reading

John 16:12-15   The Spirit reveals the truth about God
2 Corinthians 3:17-18   The Spirit transforms us

FIRE

On a sunny Spring afternoon we picnicked on a small stony beach, surrounded by steep cliffs. Someone suggested lighting a bonfire so we started to scavenge for suitable material. It wasn't difficult: wood and plastic washed up by the tide, rubbish dropped on the beach was gathered up. Soon we had the pleasure of sitting near our fire, enjoying its cheerful blaze. That fire did two things. It destroyed a lot of rubbish littering the beach, and it gave us warmth. On the first Whit Sunday God's power settled on the followers of Jesus in the form of a flame. We can think of that flame as a symbol, destroying the things that were cluttering up and spoiling the disciples' lives, by its burning making them clean again. And by its warmth kindling a flame of love and loyalty to God in them that nothing would be able to destroy. We all need the flame of God's spirit in our lives. We all need to get rid of the things that spoil our lives. And God wants to kindle a flame of love in our hearts. That flame is for sharing, and spreading the warmth of God's love to others.

Father,
    you enlighten us by your Spirit,
    so that we may know we are saved
    by your Son, Jesus Christ.
May that same Spirit inflame our hearts
    with gratitude and love,
    that our lives and our works may announce
    the Good News of salvation
    to every person we meet.
This we ask through Christ our Lord.

Amen.

For further reading

Psalm 51:10-13   The Spirit cleanses us
Acts 2:1-4   The first Pentecost

WIND

I have recently been reading a book called 'The Windmills of Kent'. I am very interested in it as it mentions two mills that I know very well, for they were bought by my great great grandfather about 150 years ago and remained in our family for several generations. The use of wind for power has been developed in various forms for many years. The power from the mills was used for grinding corn into flour and for pumping water. But during this century windmills have generally fallen into disuse, as it was thought they were not modern. But now it's being realised that we are fast using up other forms of energy, and men are again turning to the possibility of using the wind as a source of power. Today is Whit Sunday and we are reminded of the experience when the Holy Spirit of God was given to men. His coming was described as 'the sound of a mighty wind'. In other words, power came to those who loved Jesus Christ, as the Spirit came to their hearts. An inner power, that proved to be their strength in face of opposition, temptation and persecution and many other trials. You and I need that inner power to give us strength to face each day. And there is no other source apart from God's spirit. Whitsuntide is not outdated!

> **Lord Jesus Christ, in your gentleness and love**
> **breathe upon us the power of your Holy Spirit,**
> **that we may have the grace**
> **to follow you each day,**
> **wherever you may lead us.**
>
> *Amen.*

For further reading

Acts 3:1-16; 4:5-12   By what power have you done this thing?
Ephesians 3:11-21   Power in our inner being

HANDLE WITH CARE

I received a parcel recently, nothing very valuable, but the box carried a large red label saying FRAGILE, HANDLE WITH CARE. It sat in the hall for the rest of the day and I passed it every time I went in or out of the house. That word FRAGILE kept staring at me and it set me thinking how useful it would be if people wore a label saying FRAGILE when going through a difficult patch or even just having an off day. I'm sure we'd treat each other with more care and consideration. The Bible tells us of many occasions when fragile people - the sick, the blind, the lame - came to Jesus for help and none was turned away. Of course, you might say, that was 2000 years ago when Jesus was alive on earth. But what about now? Towards the end of his earthly life Jesus promised his disciples - including us - that his spirit would come and remain with us for ever. You can read about that in John's gospel, chapter 14. All through the ages since, Christians have testified to the power of this spirit and have shared their faith with one another. So even to-day we can turn to God for help and healing and what's more we can be used by him as channels of his love in all our dealings with our fellow fragile human beings

Lord Jesus Christ, my brother and friend,
 in your life and death you have shared my
 brokenness and my pain.
By the gift of your Holy Spirit,
 may I know your strength in my weakness,
 and so rise to new life with you,
 who are Lord, for ever and ever.

Amen.

For further reading

Mark 12:28-34   Love your neighbour as yourself
2 Corinthians 1:2-5   Strength and consolation to share with each other

JUNE

EXAM TIME AGAIN

It's exam time again, and many households have been supporting young people through end of term exams or GCSE or 'A' level exams which may decide their entire future. Then later on there's the ordeal of August, when results come through the letter box and everybody waits to hear the good or not so good news. Much store is set by qualifications and exam results. But although the number of GCSEs a person has may seem an easy way of judging ability, it's actually too easy. It's fine for those who do well, but what happens to those who don't or who never have the chance of gaining qualifications? Our society often makes them feel undervalued. But God doesn't have this poor attitude. He looks at people in quite another way. In fact the Bible tells us in several places not to set too much store by human knowledge alone. There are other qualifications that God looks for, particularly love and compassion. God loves everyone, whether they've got a PhD or no GCSEs at all. He has given everyone gifts, whether they are academic or not. All who are prepared to be used by God have a place in his kingdom. So, whatever your results at school may have been, remember that God values you just as you are and has given you plenty you can do for him.

> Lord I seek recognition where it cannot be found:
> In personal security
> In possessions
> In public esteem
> In status based on academic success.
> Forgive me Lord for not believing the gospel:
> You value me for what I am and
> not for what I have or for what I can do.
> Help me to accept myself as you accept me -
> because I am me.

For further reading

1 Samuel 16:1-13   The Lord does not see as man sees
Proverbs 3:5-7   Do not rely on your own understanding

PRIORITIES

Do you get cross with our climate sometimes? The weathermen promise a fine spell and down comes the rain in bucketfuls. I got caught last week. I should have known better but the sun was shining so when I went to visit a friend I wore a Summer dress. And an umbrella would have looked silly, wouldn't it? And yes, I got soaked. We can be very much like that sort of weather. Some days we find it easy to pray, enjoy reading our Bibles and find it a precious time when we gather to worship. And then how different it can be on another day. We get so involved with our busy-ness that prayers are gabbled, Bibles are skimped and somehow there is no time for God amid all the pressures of living. I should have known better about the weather. We all ought to know better, don't you agree, about our priorities in spiritual things? How wonderful that God understands and never tires of helping us back on to the right path when we turn to him, but is there waiting for us in love.

Lord I need to know you every day.
I need you as a friend with whom I walk
   and as the Lord I seek to follow.
Lord you do come to me in prayer
   if only I am willing to pray.
You come to me through scripture
   if only I will read the Bible.
Help me every day, whatever my feelings,
   to give priority to your word and to prayer.

For further reading

Isaiah 30:18-22   This is the way - follow it
1 Thessalonians 5:16-18   Keep on praying

LIFE WITHOUT GOD

I like growing runner beans - freshly picked ones taste so good! Each carefully nurtured little plant is assigned its place, with a stick ready for it to climb. Soon a slender shoot emerges. It's interesting to see how differently plants behave: some quickly find their sticks, twining closely and climbing strongly. Others need coaxing: you have to place the lengthening shoot gently round the stick before it will start climbing. Some seem to value their freedom and resist all efforts to help. They just continue to wave about defiantly. Eventually, all are climbing away, producing red flowers for the bees and, at last, succulent food for us! But suppose the little plants went completely their own way, with no stick? They wouldn't hold up for long. They would soon flop to the ground, prey to slugs and snails. If they managed to flower, the bees might miss them. Any beans that were produced would rot on the damp soil. Life without God is like that. We might like our own way, but without his support and guidance we cannot reach our full potential. Jesus told a parable about growing seeds, with a similar kind of message. You can find it in the 8th chapter of Luke's gospel.

Lord so often my life seems to lack stability.
There are days when I feel so irritable and
frustrated, days when I feel inadequate and
uncertain.
I give you thanks for being with me and
holding me firm in my moments of weakness
and doubt.
May the remembrance of your sustaining love
and constant goodness, fill me today and
tomorrow with confidence and hope.

For further reading

Micah 6:8   Walk humbly with your God
Psalm 73:23-28   Continuous close companionship

MADE IN GOD'S IMAGE

The entrance hall of the British Museum is imposing and on a June Saturday afternoon very busy. Coach parties from the provinces and family groups mingle with tourists from Japan, America, Europe. As I gazed, fascinated at this diversity of people, I became aware of a young woman at the edge of the crowd. She was behaving oddly, obviously upset. Soon I realised she was pleading for someone to help her find her child, and was astonished to find that I had moved to her side and had my arms round her. She became calmer. As the attendants relayed the message that a small child was missing, I made to leave. Immediately her panic returned, and I found myself once more putting my arms round her until she became calm. In her distress the mixture of people were just a crowd of faceless strangers and the imposing museum a place of terror. I alone seemed to offer some safety. But happily her 2 year old daughter was soon found and I continued on my way. Why am I telling you this story? Not to impress. Because, remember, I was astonished to find myself helping this woman. She was not at all like me. She was young, an African, wearing a jewel in her nose and flowing robes. She was crying out in a strange language, holding her hands out in a peculiar way, as if begging. Yet something inside me made me reach out to comfort her. We are often reminded that we are sinners, but we are not so often reminded that we are made in God's image. Which means that we have within us something of his love and this love makes us reach out, even to strangers.

> Perhaps, Lord, that's one of the many things
> that 'being made in your image' means:
> that we must take the risk of speaking to
> 'strangers'; see them as 'neighbours'.
> Help us to use the daily opportunities we
> encounter, to serve you in all and not just
> some of our brothers and sisters.

For further reading

Genesis 1:26-27   The creation of man
Luke 10:25-37   Who is my neighbour?

WHY GOD BOTHERED

God cares for me. A simple statement but what makes me believe it is true? My daily walk to the station provides me with some of the answers. At this time of the year I can't help admiring the front gardens of the houses I pass. They are ablaze with flowers, shrubs and trees. Why would God have bothered to create such beauty and colour for us to enjoy if he didn't care for us? If I leave for work early enough, I often pass a couple of dog-walkers returning from their morning walk, just a small part of the huge animal kingdom which God has created and in which we take delight. Surely a creation of someone who cares. Walking to the station on a clear Summer morning, I find myself looking up to the sky to follow the planes as they stack over Brentwood. I'm reminded of the different countries and cultures from which those planes have come. Why did God provide us with such variety? Again, isn't it because he cares about his creation? As I stand on the platform there is the usual bustle as the train approaches. As commuters we all seem to move as one. But really we are all very different. God didn't make us all the same. In his love he made us unique and of interest to each other. Through the life of Jesus most of all we can see just how much care and love God must have for us. By living among us, in Jesus, God demonstrated the central importance of love in practice, and proved that in spite of our failings, his love for us remains constant.

> **Thank you for this new day.**
> **Don't let me take for granted my freedom to**
> **stroll in your creation enjoying its colour,**
> **beauty and variety,**
> **without remembering others, deeply loved also**
> **by you, who are even at this moment locked**
> **away from the light because they**
> **acknowledge your love in Jesus.**

For further reading

Psalm 104:24-31   Who can count the things that God has made?
John 15:9-14   The central importance of love in practice

LIVING WATER

During hot dry weather it becomes increasingly evident how essential water is for life. It is not uncommon to see people concerned about their gardens out in the evenings with their hoses. I've got a hanging basket at the front of our house and have to remember to drench it thoroughly every day. Last year, when I forgot, it didn't last long and soon took on a rather shrivelled appearance. On numerous occasions in the Bible, God's work in us is likened to that of water. And when Jesus was talking to the Samaritan woman at the well he said that the water he gives is like a spring of water welling up to eternal life in a person. So it's not surprising that if we are going to survive, let alone thrive, as Christians we must get a regular drenching in God's living waters. Quite simply that means we need to spend some time with God and enjoy his company so that he may refresh our spirits. King David, the psalmist, used to 'pant for God's presence like a thirsty deer.' Do we? If, on the other hand we deprive our souls of this living water it won't be too long before it begins to show. We will begin to feel spiritually dry and barren and I'm sure others will begin to notice a shrivelled-ness about us! Let's make sure then, that we get a drenching, spiritually speaking, as often as possible.

> **I suppose you smile at our anti-wrinkle creams
>   and skin fresheners.
> But with the smile of a father who knows.
> Direct me towards all that deep cleanses my
>   heart, moisturises my mind and makes my
>   spirit supple enough to stretch into the vast
>   dimensions of your love.**

For further reading

Psalm 42:1-2   Thirst for God
John 4:1-15; 7:37-39   An inner spring, welling up

FRAGRANCE

A few months ago, back in the winter time, we were planning to buy some rose bushes. We studied the catalogue and talked about what colours we should have and noted how each variety was described. We were particularly interested in the scented ones. "The fragrance is absolutely magnificent," it said of one. Another one was "delightfully fragrant." We wanted sweet-scented roses as well as lovely colours. The Bible says that the life of a Christian has fragrance. St. Paul once wrote: "Thanks be to God who, in Christ, always leads us in triumph and through us spreads the fragrance of the knowledge of him everywhere." One thing I notice is that he doesn't say that we are to try and spread fragrance, but it is something the Lord does through those who love him. A life that is centred in him has a beauty and fragrance which spreads everywhere around. Perhaps you are placed in circumstances which make it difficult for you to do much in the way of active service for him. You cannot perhaps witness as you would like to do. But take heart. He can still use you if you keep close to him. You may not know that you are having any influence at all, but your life can be fragrant with his joy and love and the Lord will be blessing others through you.

I wonder if people feel better for meeting me?
More energetic? Or are they drained?
Lord, help me.
I'd like to pass on more of you and less of me.
Please help me, Lord.

For further reading

Ephesians 4:32; 5:1-2   Try to be like him
Philippians 4:4-9   Something to think about!

GOD IN EVERYTHING

There's a very famous hymn in the Bible, in Psalm 139, which talks about God being absolutely everywhere: "If I go to the highest mountain top you are there. If I go down into the depths of the sea, you are there." We know in our heads that it's true. But what about feeling it in our hearts? And what if we aren't up mountains or on the sea bed but stuck in the office on a hot day or queuing in Sainsbury's? Jesus Christ said of himself, "I am Truth." And I believe that when we discover the real truth about ourselves and learn to accept it and get on with it, we meet Christ in our own experience. I was very struck recently with the story of a young monk who asked his master in the monastery for some spiritual instruction. "Have you had breakfast?" asked the master. "Yes, thank you," replied the monk. "Then go and wash the dishes," said the master. Facing up to reality, then tackling the next job that needs to be done is perhaps a much more significant happening than most of us realise, for if God is present in everything, it is in everything that we find him.

I have to confess, Lord, I find it difficult to
realise that you are in Sainsbury's.
Perhaps that means I want to confine you to
Galilee or even to Gothic buildings.
But 'Emmanuel' means 'God with us'.
Forgive me, Lord, and help me to grow in
understanding as well as in faith.

For further reading

Psalm 16:7-11 Joy in God's presence
1 Peter 4:10-11 Do everything you do as if for God

Hello! This is MESSAGE...

SUMMER HOLIDAYS

THE SILLY SEASON

The other day I heard August being referred to as 'the silly month'. It reminded me of a former boss of mine who used to call it 'the silly season'. It's true: things are somewhat different in August: people go away on holiday, clubs and organisations close down till September, that sort of thing. At home, at present, we have a relief milkman and a relief postman! I thought I would look up the word 'silly' in my old school dictionary. It says 'foolish, thoughtless, harmless, innocent, imprudent': quite a variety, I think you will agree. And 'silly season' is actually mentioned there, as the time when newspapers start trivial discussions because of lack of news. But some things don't ever change: we still have to pay the gas bill and buy food. And one piece of substantial, unchanging news is that God remains constant, steadfast, and loving and we cannot be separated from him. God does not go away on holidays or have a silly season. If we look up John's gospel, chapter 6, we find Peter - one of the disciples - saying, "Lord, to whom else would we go? You have the words that give eternal life. And now we believe and know that you are the holy one who has come from God." Nothing silly (in any of its definitions) about those words.

> Lord, this may be a 'silly season' to some folk,
>   but I have real issues to face today, real
>   problems to solve.
> Save me from triviality and help me focus on
>   the urgent matters that need my attention.
> With your help, I believe I can make this a
>   problem-solving day.
> May it be so.
>
> *Amen.*

For further reading

Isaiah 40:25-31   God doesn't get weary
John 6:66-69   Words of eternal life

DEEP PEACE

When we are tired or anxious it sometimes helps to go on a journey. I want to take you in imagination to the west coast of Scotland. When we get there a small boat will take us to the island of Iona. Iona is the cradle of Scottish Christianity. It is a quiet place: the sea, the earth, the stars. The air seems full of faith, a faith that has built up since St. Columba first brought the Christian good news from Ireland in the year 563. Each year, on June 9th, we remember St. Columba especially. As we explore this lovely island, I want to share with you some words that are often used by Christian people on Iona to-day. They are words about the peace of God. Here they are:

> "Deep peace of the running wave to you.
> Deep peace of the flowing air to you.
> Deep peace of the quiet earth to you.
> Deep peace of the shining stars to you.
> Deep peace of the Son of Peace to you."

These are words for us. We have to go back to our everyday lives, but we go in the peace of God.

**Lord, help me to discover the peace you offer in
the unexpected places that are all around me.
In my friendships.
In my journeying.
In my reading.
In a brief moment of complete quietness.**
Amen.

For further reading

Isaiah 26:3-4   Trust in the Lord
John 14:27   The parting gift of Jesus

DEEP LOVE

How deep is the love of Christ? Here's a summer story which helps to point to an answer: On one of the lovely beaches of the Isle of Wight, a small boy was playing with his inflatable boat. His father had pumped it up for him and he staggered down to the water's edge with his treasured possession. He looked back at his parents in triumph as he floated his boat in a few inches of water. It was low tide and there was hardly a ripple on the sea. Then the boy climbed into the boat, put his arms out and tried to push himself along. But the weight of his body had pushed the boat into the sand. It would not budge. He jumped out, saw that it now floated, and climbed back in, only to find himself stuck again. He got out, carried the boat back to his father and said, "It's no good Daddy, the water isn't deep enough!" Those within hearing smiled, for a 25,000 ton liner had sailed majestically past only minutes before. I recognise myself in that little boy. Don't we sometimes take our problems to the edge of Christ's love and then say, "It's no good. His love isn't deep enough to meet my need." Perhaps that's why The Lord Jesus had to say to his disciples, "Launch out into the deep." The love of Christ has proved deep enough for millions of people down through the years. And many people to-day would confirm that his love can meet their deepest need. He waits to share that love with us all.

> Lord, I acknowledge that I have too often been
> content to sample the shallows of your loving
> purpose for me.
> Give me courage to launch out into the deep
> this day, to let the moorings go and trust you
> with matters I have, till now, sought to
> resolve in my own limited strength.
>
> *Amen.*

For further reading

Matthew 11:28-30   Relief for your souls
Romans 11:33-36   Source, guide and goal of all that is

DEEP PIT

A few weeks ago I spent a week's holiday in a canal boat. The countryside is very hilly around Cheshire and in navigating the canals it is necessary to go through a large number of locks. One day when I was steering the boat I drove into what proved to be a very deep lock. As the boat went in, the deep murky sides of the lock blotted out all the sunshine. They completely enclosed the boat in what felt like a deep, dark pit. After the gates had been shut, the paddles at the other end were raised and the water rose rapidly lifting the boat nearer and nearer the light and the warmth of the sun. Whilst watching this happening I was struck by the thought that there are times in most people's lives - and I include myself - when we feel we are at the bottom of a dark pit and that all around us is blackness. And there doesn't seem to be any way in which we can climb out. My boat didn't get out of the lock by itself. It was able to rise up from the darkness into the light because the water came in underneath and lifted it up. Water is very powerful and easily raises the weight of a 70 foot boat. Jesus often spoke of the power given to him by God. "All power is given unto me in heaven and on earth." His power was not used to beat people down, but rather to raise them up. To heal those who were sick, to bring comfort to the sad, to show God's love to all around him. And if that's where you feel you are now, in a dark pit, can I ask you to try to stop worrying that you can't get out in your own strength. But God's power can do it, as the water lifted my boat out into the sunshine again. I'd like to encourage you to trust him to do it.

> Lord, I own my weakness, my inability to be
>   what I long to be, to do what I should be
>   doing.
> Come to me with strong evidence of your
>   nearness, and do for me just now what I can
>   never do for myself.
> I trust you for this, Lord.
>
> > *Amen.*

For further reading

Psalm 18:1-6   I cried to God for help
Nahum 1:7   God is our refuge in time of distress

MESSAGE IN A DECKCHAIR

I've sat in a deck chair many times, but it was only recently that I learnt of its origin, when I read about Edward Atkins. One hundred years ago he went up to London to set up in business making furniture. For fifteen years it was hard going. Then, one summer, Edward made a folding chair for his wife to use in the garden. It was simply made, just a few pieces of wood and some canvas. Friends saw the chair, admired it, and Edward was encouraged to make more. He took six to Margate where they were hired out on the beach. They were an immediate success and orders came flooding in. Soon, thousands of deck chairs were in use on ocean liners. Every summer, on beaches, in parks and in many back gardens they can be seen. It all began when Edward Atkins made a present for the wife he loved. A gift for one person became a welcome item of relaxation and comfort for many. It's not often that one person's gift multiplies to the benefit of countless people. But that's exactly what happened when God gave his gift of Jesus. One child born 2000 years ago into one family was destined to become the source and continuing provider of comfort and strength, victory and new life to all who accepted him.

> **Lord, I have gifts.**
> **Help me to discover them, possibly a very**
> **practical gift using my hands, possibly a**
> **literary gift writing letters, or perhaps the gift**
> **of encouragement.**
> **And help me to place my gift at your service, in**
> **some way, this very day.**
> *Amen.*

For further reading

Romans 3:22-30   God's design in Jesus
Psalm 23:1-6   Goodness and unfailing love

FOLLOW ME

I imagine you probably live in a built-up area like me. And perhaps you enjoy going to 'be beside the seaside'. Maybe the final summer Bank Holiday that's coming up will afford you such an opportunity. I like to recall the glimpse I had of the Sea of Galilee, once referred to as the loveliest lake in the world. It is small - only 13 by 8 miles - its surface is below sea level, in a genial climate with beautiful surrounding hilly countryside. Its gentle waves are only disturbed when sudden storms beat down from between the hills. On these shores Jesus issued his call to Peter and Andrew and others - "Follow me." These fishermen tied up their boats, left their families and set out on a life that would prove to be a great spiritual adventure, which in time would be marked with the cross. And on the way these men worked many wonders. I am reminded of the popular hymn "Dear Lord and Father of Mankind" which we sang as our boat dropped anchor half way across the sea: "In simple trust like theirs who heard beside the Syrian sea the gracious calling of the Lord, let us, like them, without a word, rise up and follow thee." Jesus worked wonders through ordinary men and women, and still the call rings out, "Follow me." Perhaps he is calling us.

> Lord, I will hear many voices this day, each
> summoning my attention or demanding my
> response.
> May I keep my ears tuned for your voice this
> day.
> Your 'follow me'.
> And, when I hear it, may I be willing to obey.
> *Amen.*

For further reading

Luke 19:1-10   Jesus works wonders through ordinary people
John 10:27-28   The call of his familiar voice

DO NOT BE AFRAID

Looking through some old holiday photos the other day, I recalled my time spent in the Lake District. A favourite outing in the evening was a trip to the cinema. But the times of the buses hadn't been designed for cinema goers and we always arrived after the film had started. What's more the second showing of the main feature was still going on when we had to leave to catch our bus back home. And as a result, we got used to seeing the end first and then the beginning. Sometimes we wish life could be like that. When times are tough or we are starting on a new venture, it would be helpful to know how things will turn out before we start. (Though, at the cinema we often found it frustrating!) But, to be honest, I'm sure life wouldn't be nearly as interesting or challenging if we knew the future. There is one thing, though, that we can be sure of. God is in control and he is with us. I'd like to share with you some words of Jesus that have helped me when I felt I'd like to know the future, and needed an injection of courage: "In this life you will have trouble, but take heart! Do not be afraid! I have overcome the world," and "I will be with you till the end of time."

> Lord, if I have spent too much time recently
>   worrying about the future, help me this day
>   to place the unknown tomorrow in your
>   hands.
> I do so consciously at this moment.
> I pledge myself to live 'one step at a time'.
> I feel my faith growing even as I offer this
>   prayer to you, my loving Lord.
> *Amen.*

For further reading

Psalm 26:1-3   Unfaltering trust in the Lord
1 Corinthians 15:55-58   Death is swallowed up in victory

AUTUMN & HARVEST

FILLING THE EMPTINESS

September is often a month when 'things get going again'. Clubs and societies start their programme, evening classes begin. I heard this phrase recently and it stuck in my mind: "A dizzy whirl around a central emptiness." It stuck because it seemed to express the inner state of a good many of us. "A dizzy whirl around a central emptiness." I tried to think it out. "A dizzy whirl?" - not necessarily wrong. Most of us live in some sort of a whirl in our fast-moving age. "Around a central emptiness?" That's not good. Even a moth whirls round something! A light. But we whirl, many of us, around nothing. There's nothing to centre our life on. We look for it hastily sometimes, as we whirl. But the centre is empty. We need something, someone, to be sure of, something secure, that stays, that understands - that loves! Is that asking too much? No. God has made us the way we are - searching, whirling humans, and he has provided a centre for us where we find these needs met. St. Paul knew by experience, many of us know it too, that our central emptiness can be filled. Filled by the living Christ. "Christ in you - you in Christ." Here is certainty, a person, a centre.

Dear Lord, we rightly involve ourselves, to do
our best for this finite world, but this can
never wholly satisfy us because we are made
eternal in your image.
Help us to acknowledge our deepest needs and
longings and to know that they can be satisfied only by knowing you.

For further reading

Ephesians 2:17-22 Jesus: the foundation stone
Colossians 2:6-10 Rooted and built up in him

GROWING OLDER, STAYING YOUNG

Have you ever got up in the morning, looked in the bathroom mirror and been shocked at what you saw? Even more shocked than usual, that is! Look, there's a grey hair there! A wrinkle there! My hair's receding! I'm getting old! Even more alarming: have you met up with an old friend you haven't seen for years? "My word," you exclaim, "you haven't changed a bit!" But what you're thinking is, "Doesn't he or she look old! And they're the same age as me!" It's very hard, isn't it for us to accept that from the time that we are born we are starting to get older. Some of us have trouble coping with aging. We try to cover up the effects with make-up, wigs, hair-dye. It's all rather pointless. We can't stop the process, or even slow it down, much less start again. But in our spiritual life it's quite a different story. When St. Paul was writing to the new Christians in Corinth, he encouraged them like this: "Even though our physical being is gradually decaying, yet our spiritual being is renewed day after day. For we fix our attention not on the things that are seen, but on the things that are unseen. What can be seen lasts only for a time, but what cannot be seen lasts for ever." No matter how young or how old we are in the faith, we can be renewed each day. Instead of mourning our lost youth we can concentrate our thinking on the newness of our spiritual being each day and look beyond our frail humanity.

"Dear Lord and father of mankind, forgive our
    foolish ways!"
Renew my long-term vision, my long-term
    faith, my longterm hope, my longterm joy,
    for your kingdom's sake.

For further reading
Psalm 103:1-5   Youth ever new
John 3:1-8   New birth, spiritually speaking

OUR LAST DAY

I've been thinking lately about time. When one's a child one seems to have all the time in the world. Waiting for Christmas Eve to come seemed endless. As I get older time flies past. Do you remember the story Jesus told of the man who had amassed great wealth after a super harvest. He decided to build a vast barn to hold his treasure and settle down to a life of ease and plenty. God said to him, "You foolish man. This night your soul will be required of you ." None of us knows how long we've got here on earth - probably that's a good thing! However, without intending to be at all morbid, if we did know that this was our last week on earth, what a difference it would make. I'm sure it would make us intensely aware of the world around us and give us the desire not to fritter the precious moments way. Maybe it wouldn't be a bad thing to live each day as if it were our last!

> As each day comes with its blessings and
>   difficulties, opportunities and frustrations,
>   it's often not easy to feel fully alive to what is
>   going on, and to long for a peaceful, future
>   time.
> Lord, make me more sensitive to the richness of
>   today, rather than yearning for a tomorrow
>   which may never come.

For further reading

Deuteronomy 8:11-18   Watch out, if you get wealthy!
Luke 12:13-40   Where your treasure is, there will your heart be also

LOOK AT THE EVIDENCE

The sky was bright blue, and almost cloudless. It was a most unusual day for mid October and so greatly appreciated. I was drinking a cup of tea when Alan asked, "Can you see that plane up there?" Across the sky were two curved white lines, which we recognised as the evidence of a plane. But although we looked intently, the plane could not be seen. God too has left evidence of his presence in our world, and although our eyes cannot see him, there is no doubt that he is there. There is the sky, and the sea, vast expanses which speak of his power. But, too, there are the small things which tell of the delicacy of his touch. The hand is more wonderful than any machine. The brain more wonderful than any computer. Look around you. You may not see God himself, but there is plenty of evidence of his creative hand. I'd like to quote from one of my favourite psalms: Psalm 19. "How clearly the sky reveals God's glory! How plainly it shows what he has done. Each day announces it to the following day, each night repeats it to the next. No speech or words are used, no sound is heard, yet their message goes out to all the world and is heard to the ends of the earth."

Your creation, my God, is good and wonderful. Renew my sense of wonder, delight and reverence for all that surrounds me, for all that I am, and for the new understandings of your power which are constantly revealed to us by advances in science and technology.

For further reading

Acts 14:8-17   Plenty of clues
Hebrews 11:1-3   Invisible, but clearly seen

SAY THANK YOU

It's easy for us living in this temperate country, where there have never been terrible excesses of heat or cold, or earthquake or volcanic eruptions, to see a pattern in the changing crops and seasons. Night following day. Summer after spring, seeds sown and almost always developing into plants as we had hoped. But for the people living in countries where these things can't be taken for granted, a real problem! When they see crops fail, floods devastate their lands and wash away not only seeds but also homes and whole villages, where life is still desperately hard, often short, always unpredictable, it's little wonder that they leave trays of flowers and sweets outside their houses and shops to implore the evil spirits not to strike. We can't put ourselves in their place if we haven't lived in countries with such conditions. Shouldn't this make us even more deeply and humbly thankful for the good things we take for granted? We have in no way deserved them, yet, because of where we live, it happens to be our privilege. Do we give thanks to God for his faithfulness to us? He promised that "while the earth remains seedtime and harvest shall not fail." But we rarely give him a thought. This is a good time of year to sharpen up our awareness of the daily blessings we receive from our God.

Praise the Lord!
I woke up this morning.
My heart is still beating!
It's the gift of another day.
Praise the Lord!

For further reading
1 Chronicles 29:10-13   Thanks for daily blessings
Psalm 8:1-9   What an amazing world!

LISTEN

I once went to a church service in the middle of October when the preacher's first words were: "A happy Easter to you!" Adults and children alike stared at him in amazement, but he was right. It was Sunday. And every Sunday can be Easter Sunday when we remember that Jesus is alive and with us now. Many years ago my husband and I were homeless and desperate for shelter. A very kind lady took us into her home and showed us a love we had not known. It was Easter time and she invited me to go with her to Church. That evening Jesus spoke to me, calling me by name and saying, "I died for you." And the experience has changed my whole life. Now God has given me the opportunity and privilege of going some way to repaying that lady. She is 93, almost blind, and in a nursing home. And in the time I am able to spend with her I try to give her the love she gave me all those years ago. If you only go to Church occasionally, why not go this Sunday and listen to what God may have to say, personally, to you. I pray that you, too, will have the joy, love and peace that that Sunday evening has brought me all these many years.

> God of life, God of grace, help me not only to
> welcome opportunities to serve others but
> also to receive with thankfulness the love that
> others offer to me.

For further reading

Romans 12:9-16   Warmth of mutual affection
1 Corinthians 15:1-7   The historical facts of Easter

GOD'S MULTIPLICATION

For to-day's message, I'd like to give you two sentences. The first was something a friend of mine remarked this week: "God's favourite branch of mathematics is multiplication." Harvest time is the ideal time to see what he meant: a complete field of wheat from just a small bag of seeds. Outside my back door in June, I planted a couple of manky looking shrivelled up corms, and now you can scarcely get down the path to hang out the washing for the dahlias tumbling everywhere. The second sentence was something said to a beggar by one of the first followers of Jesus: "Silver and gold have I none, but such as I have, I give to you." You know, I often hear myself saying, "I can't do anything to help in that situation," or, "I don't have the gifts needed for that." But the Bible makes it quite clear that we aren't expected by God to give what we haven't got, but we are supposed to say, "What I have got, I give you." We don't need to hold back from giving what we have to others because we think it's too small. God can multiply its value, but only if we give it first. A letter perhaps, a visit, a compliment even, a smile, an offer of help, a word of encouragement. God can do great things from small beginnings .

> **God, my creator, help me to recognise the gifts you have entrusted to me for service in this world.**
> **Give me the courage to offer them where they are needed, confident that when I do I shall be touching the world with your power, a power which knows no limits.**

For further reading

Matthew 25:14-29   A parable about making the most of your talents
Mark 6:30-44   The feeding of the five thousand

YOU'D NEVER GUESS

Always in September I buy some daffodil and hyacinth bulbs and plant them in pots ready for flowering in January. January is a cold and sometimes dreary month and these beautiful flowers give great pleasure. I am always fascinated by the contrast between the rather dull, dead-looking bulb which I plant and the colourful flower that comes from it. If you hadn't ever seen a daffodil there's no way you could guess what it would be like by looking at the bulb! Sometimes people get quite worried, wondering what life will be like in the next world. What will we look like? How will we recognise each other? Will we in fact exist at all? I think, you know, that talking and worrying like that is rather like looking at the daffodil bulb and trying to guess from it what the flower will be like. It can't be done! St. Paul says that "on earth we have an earthly body and in heaven we shall have a heavenly body." So don't let's allow it to worry us. We are in God's hands. He has much more splendid bodies in mind than we can possibly imagine. And looking at the daffodils, I think we can confidently leave the matter right there!

> Lord, you have promised that all things will be
> brought to perfection in your kingdom.
> Let me rest in the confidence of knowing that
> by your power, after death, all our weakness
> and frailty will be transformed into
> wholeness and beauty beyond our imagining.

For further reading

Jeremiah 17:7-8   Just trust!
1 John 4:17-19   Perfect love casts out fear

Hello! This is MESSAGE...

THE BEGINNING
OF WINTER

THE PROBLEM OF WAKING UP

I wonder how good you are at getting up in the morning. I must admit that on these dark mornings now, I have to rely on an extremely loud alarm clock to wake me from sleep. And for many people, waking up is the hardest thing they have to do all day. But is waking up all that bad? Do you remember an occasion when you were so excited the night before you could hardly go to sleep? Perhaps it was Christmas Eve, or the night before going on holiday. Whatever it was, I'm sure you woke up quickly that morning. So maybe the answer to the problem of trying to wake up in the morning is to anticipate that God will have something special in store for you each day. Then you will not be able to resist waking up easily. Catch the excitement of the Psalmist who said: "This is the day which the Lord has made. Let us rejoice and be glad in it." Suddenly the day will take on a new perspective.

Lord I know that however I start the new day it is your gift.
Whether I wake slowly or quickly let there be an early point in every day when I remember it is yours, and not mine.
I come into it as a co-creator with you of the better world you desire.
Let me so wake with thanks that on the strength of the day I may be also able to end it with gratitude, through Jesus Christ Our Lord.

Amen

For further reading

Psalm 130:5-8   The morning watchman greets the day
Ephesians 1:15-22   Catch some of Paul's excitement!

HEAVY BURDENS

I had a rather odd experience last week. It was a typical November evening, dark, damp and a bit foggy. I felt something brush the front of my car as I was driving home. Perhaps a bird, I thought. But I saw and heard nothing. So I drove on. But yesterday, driving to town past the same spot, I caught sight of one of those yellow police notices on an easel. All day I worried about it. What if it hadn't been a bird? What if I had hit a child? I felt I was carrying a heavy weight. As soon as I got back I hurried to read the notice. It said: "Don't park this side. Highway maintenance in progress." The weight I needn't have carried dropped off. Most of us at times carry burdens around. Maybe worries. Maybe guilt. Maybe unnecessarily! The yellow-notice episode reminded me of something the Bible says about Jesus: "He has carried the weight of our suffering, the burden that should have been ours has been laid on him." This is something of a mystery. It seems certainly to refer to Jesus on the cross, but it also describes the sort of strength and encouragement and peace of mind that is available through prayer. I don't know what your beliefs are or whether you are even at this moment carrying a heavy burden of some kind, or even a relatively trivial concern. My own belief is that the cross of Christ is the best place to go in search of strength and help.

> Oh God I thank you that at the heart of the Christian
> message there is forgiveness for sins and the lifting of
> burdens because of your love for us through Jesus
> Christ.
> Forgive me that I so easily bring to you my burden and
> then carry it away again!
> Help me today truly to lay my burdens down at your
> feet, and to walk away free to serve you, through Jesus
> Christ Our Lord.
>
> *Amen*

For further reading

Micah 7:18-19   God deals with our guilt
Colossians 2:13-15   Sins forgiven

WE NEED EACH OTHER

I'm a bit old fashioned and still prefer an open fire. Every night during the winter before going to bed, I take out some of the top unburnt coals and lay them on the hearth so that they don't continue to burn away, and I use them again next day. Sometimes of course the fire is so hot that even with the tongs I can't get close enough to take out more than just the top few lumps. And yet, as soon as they have been removed, within a few minutes they have gone dull and lost their former glow. And that's a good illustration of how our lives can stop 'glowing' and 'go black'. And often, this is because we need the company and help of other people. No doubt you will know the story of Adam in the Garden of Eden, and how God looked everywhere among the animals to find company for him. But it was not until God created Eve that Adam's need for society and help was satisfied. He needed another human being like himself. Perhaps it was this thought that was in the mind of the writer to the Hebrews when he said "Let us not give up meeting together, as some are in the habit of doing, but let us encourage one another." It is a plain and simple fact that friendship and fellowship with others can quickly restore the 'glow' to our lives.

> Thank you, Father, that in your family the Church there
> is warmth and light and renewal for all of us.
> Help me Lord not only to ensure that I myself am
> strengthened and warmed through that fellowship, but
> that also within that fellowship I look out for those
> who are the shy and the lonely, the hesitant and the
> withdrawn.
> Coals can't draw other coals towards them, but humans
> can!
> Help me to draw others into the warmth of your love
> today, I pray, through Jesus Christ Our Lord.
>
> *Amen*

For further reading

Genesis 2:15-25   It is not good to be alone
Acts 2:42-47   The fellowship of the church

JESUS NEEDS US!

St. Andrew is particularly remembered on November 30th. He was one of the friends of Jesus on earth. He was a fisherman on Lake Galilee, like his brother Simon Peter, and the brothers James and John. We don't know much about Andrew, except that he brought people to Jesus. When he first met Jesus, he fetched his brother to meet him too. It was that brother, Simon Peter, who became a close companion to Jesus, but Andrew showed no resentment. Later on it was Andrew who brought to Jesus the lad who offered his picnic lunch to help feed a great crowd. Andrew didn't think the five rolls and two fish would be much use, but he trusted Jesus. On another day some Greeks wanted to meet Jesus, and asked Philip, another disciple, to introduce them. He referred them to Andrew. Would Jesus want to meet foreigners? Andrew had no doubts. He brought them to Jesus. That's really all we know about Andrew, just one of the backroom boys really, like most of us. Jesus needed him, as he needs us, to do his work.

> **Lord, how wonderful to have the reputation that the**
> **main thing people remembered about you was that**
> **you brought other people to Jesus!**
> **Some of us find that easier than others, but we can all be**
> **part of the processes in other people's lives by which**
> **they come nearer to you.**
> **Lord I don't know what part you wish me to play in**
> **helping others to come to you, but I say today that,**
> **like Andrew, I'm ready, through Jesus Christ Our Lord.**
> *Amen*

For further reading

Jeremiah 1:4-9   He needs us to do his work
Matthew 4:18-22   Andrew responds to the call of Jesus

MAKING TRACKS

It has been snowing all morning. When I walked up the garden my boots left large holes in the deep snow. I saw tracks where our cat had been. And others, not so deep, left by the birds. It was quite evident where I had been. Every step was clear. Our daily steps, too, are evident, even when there is no snow. Our attitude, pleasant or grumbling, affects us, ourselves, and our neighbours and everyone we meet during the day. Our words can have a lasting effect. Whether they were kind or not. It's snowing again. In a short while my tracks will have disappeared. There are also tracks in my life that I would like to blot out. There are words I wish I had not said, or even thought. God has promised that if we admit our mistakes and are truly sorry and are willing to forgive others, we can be forgiven. King David, the same David who wrote the 23rd Psalm, "The Lord is my Shepherd," also once (or maybe many times!) offered this prayer: "Create in me a clean heart, O God, wash me and I shall be whiter than snow." Most of us are not unlike David, so we can make his prayer our own.

> **Lord if today lies ahead of me like an unbroken expanse
> of snow, may my tracks be good and clear for you.
> Let them walk to those who are in greatest need, and let
> every part of the journey be towards you.
> And if others should be watching my tracks today, please
> let every part of the way that I plot out give help to
> them in their search for everything that's good and
> lovely and true, so that they too may walk towards
> you, through Jesus Christ Our Lord.**
>
> *Amen*

For further reading
Proverbs 15:1-4   I wish I hadn't said that...
1 John 1:5-10   ...but I'm ready to admit I was wrong

ADVENT

DISPELLING THE DARKNESS

December always seems to me to be the busiest month of the year. It is also one of the darkest months. But most of the darkness can be dispelled by thoughts of what Christmas really means. The birthday of the one who came to be the light of the world. The practical preparations for this event seem to begin earlier every year. But I ask myself sometimes whether there is as much spiritual preparation. Do we stop sometimes in our activities to be thankful for the coming of Jesus? For all it meant, and means and will mean! Jesus was born at a time when there was very similar strife to that which we have to-day. Yet the Bethlehem baby became the teacher who taught the way of peace. He spoke of feeding the hungry, visiting prisoners, healing the sick, caring for widows and fatherless. And his whole life was one of selfless service. And he left us his 'in-as-much-as' message: "In as much as" we serve others in these ways, we are truly serving, him. Can we light up this dull December by pondering upon these truths in a deeper way? And as we ourselves find deeper faith, so we shall be ready to re-dedicate ourselves for the service of those around us who are in need. This, I'm convinced, is the way to personal freedom. To be set free from all fretting self-concern, to care for others. To see Jesus in them. The light and hope of the world.

Lord, soon we will celebrate your birth in Bethlehem in a cattle shed.

Forgive us that still today children are born in poverty.

Forgive us that so many this Christmas time will be cold and lonely.

We pray for: homeless people seeking shelter, unemployed people wanting work, hungry people needing food, parents crying for their children.

Give us the spirit of compassion so that all will have the opportunity for a full and fulfilling life.

For further reading

Isaiah 9:2-7   The people who walked in darkness have seen a great light

John 1:1-9   The light shines on in the darkness

MONEY WORRIES AT CHRISTMAS

Christmas is usually pictured as the time of joy and laughter. If you're like me it's not as simple as that. It's often full of all sorts of worries as well, not least the concern about where all the extra money is to be found to buy the things that the adverts try to convince us that children, friends and relatives will want from us at Christmas time. How are we going to make the little we have stretch to buy all the things we need to get? If we believed all we heard, we'd think that no-one worried about money to-day and that it was a get-rich-quick type of world we live in. I remember once being sent down the road to buy a present with one of those old threepenny pieces. I got to the end of the road, tripped over the kerb and dropped the coin down the drain. I felt like trying to hitch a lift to China rather than go home to face the family with the news that I had lost the money. Well, if we listen too much to the world, we shall indeed be bothered about how much we have or haven't got. But maybe, if we listen instead to the words of Isaiah, we shall remember that Christmas is about God, who gives without price, who comes without cost and who loves without any thought of what we should give to him. These words say: "Come to the waters, you who are thirsty and let him who has no money come buy and eat. Come, buy wine and milk without price." You do not need to budget for the real gift of Christmas. Jesus is God's greatest gift to every one of us.

> Lord, Bethlehem was unprepared for your coming, and that is how it is with me.
> I've presents to buy, cards to send, food to prepare.
> Help!
> Help me to stop and consider my priorities.
> Help me to pause and think about the deeper meaning of your birth.
> May I realize that the joy of Christmas is not dependent on my financial resources but rather on knowing and accepting your love freely offered to me.
> Help me to receive this precious gift with gratitude.

For further reading

Isaiah 55:1-5   Why spend money on things that don't satisfy?
Ephesians 2:4-8   Jesus is God's free gift to us

CHRISTMAS CARDS

One of the Christmas customs that seems to be getting out of hand in our family is the sending of Christmas cards. We seem to send and receive more and more each year. The people we send cards to tend to fall into two groups. The first group is people we see regularly, perhaps every day at work, for example, but whom we feel obliged to send to and who may be offended, we feel, if we don't. The second group are friends of the past whom we never see now but like to keep in touch with once a year in this way. It's easy to have a 'Christmas card' relationship with God in the same two ways. We know that the main way we can communicate with God is through prayer, and yet it's easy, if we pray at all regularly to fall into the trap of doing so out of a sense of duty, a fear of offending God if we don't pray, rather than a true love for him and a desire to know him better. The other way of having a 'Christmas card' relationship with God is to offer the occasional prayer, perhaps in church, just to 'keep in touch'. The greatest commandment Jesus gave us was to love God, and we can't love someone we don't know. The way to know and love God is to turn to him each day, to share with him all our hopes and fears, our joys and sorrows, and to ask him to give us the help, support and encouragement of a true friend. My wife and I are going to try and see some of our 'Christmas card' friends this year to renew our friendship on a deeper level. Perhaps we should resolve to renew our relationship with God too.

Lord in my better moments, I know that nothing stands in the way of your love.
There will never be a time when your love for me will end.
When I fall you lift me up.
Forgive me for my moments of doubt.
Help me to respond to your faithful love by a deeper commitment to you.
May my faith in you be
- more than a passing interest, fitted grudgingly into a busy timetable,
- more than a crutch to lean on when other things have failed.
Rather may my heart be renewed by the strength of your constant love.

For further reading

Psalm 63:1-8   A real longing for a deeper relationship with God
Luke 11:1-8   Lord, teach us how to pray

THE SEASON OF GOODWILL

Do you ever stop to think about some of the things we say to each other at Christmas? We make the same comments, use the same phrases year after year, until they become part of a ritual and we say them with little thought. Opening a Christmas card, I read: "Best wishes for this season of goodwill." Now, nothing unusual about that, but, for the first time, the phrase 'season of goodwill' really struck me. I thought: "Do the wishes not continue when the season is over?" Oh, I know what's meant, but the idea of 'a season of goodwill' jarred with me and still does. Does it mean that for a few days we try to be nice to each other, kinder, more considerate, and then return to being our normal selves? This is sometimes what we expect. We expect compassion and sympathy at Christmas more than at other times of the year. Is it asking too much of human nature to extend its goodwill throughout the year, rather than just for a season? I suspect we are touching the root of the problem of our living together. Our goodwill to others so often is just seasonal. It comes and goes, depending upon our mood and what sort of day we've had. The essential message of Christmas is of eternal goodwill - of God's love to us for ever, and not just for a season. It's a promise that he will stand by us always. And in the strength of that companionship we are bound to cultivate an attitude of year-round goodwill to 'all mankind'. And that must include the family next door.

Some of us remember wartime 'rationing'.
Is that what we do with our love?
Lord have mercy.
Christ have mercy.
Lord have mercy.

For further reading

Romans 13:8-10   Love is what it's all about
Hebrews 13:1-2   So don't ever stop loving

I DID IT MY WAY

Have you heard that song 'My Way'? Silly question, really. It was that colossal hit that kept Frank Sinatra in the charts for weeks. Apparently it's a very popular last choice for playing at funerals. Can you imagine passing from this life and standing before God and saying "I did it my way!"? 'My way' is as old as Creation itself. Adam and Eve are portrayed as saying they'd do it 'their way'. And that sentiment has been echoed right down through history into the 20th century. And the fulfilment of it can be seen in any newspaper - countries ravaged by war, indiscriminate bombings, pollution, perversion, murder and rape. History indeed groans with the fact that Man has done it 'his way'. There's a verse in the Bible that says, "There is a way that seems right to man, but it ends in death." That's the 'my way' that has led to separation from God. But thank God - he has counteracted the 'my way' philosophy with his own 'God's way.' The end of this month of December reminds us of 'God's way.' Jesus came, that Christmas 2000 years ago, to show us 'God's way'. He came to destroy death and bring life, and deal with the 'my way' mentality that gripped humanity. And he didn't do it on a vague, general level but on a personal level. He died for me and for you personally and looks for a personal response from each of us. The approach of Christmas should prompt us to reconsider the way we are taking. Is it God's way for us?

> So often we look in despair at the world of
>   fighting men and women, and say, "Surely
>   there must be a better way than this!"
> Thank God, there is!

For further reading

Isaiah 55:7-9   God's ways are not our ways
Hebrews 2:14-15   He came to destroy death

CHRISTMAS

EMMANUEL

I went to see a play recently and it began with a prayer. 'Pretty unusual play!' you may be thinking. Not everyone's cup of tea. But you'd be wrong. It was at the National Theatre and all the seats were sold. As the lights went down one actor stood in the spotlight. He was playing the part of a country vicar. And he prayed: "Lord. Are you there?" And that's something that most people ask at some time, however strong their faith. "Where are you, God?" It's quite difficult sometimes to feel that God is with us. But I'm sure that it's a bit like when you lose your keys and you're hunting all over the place and often you're staring right at them but somehow you don't see them. But if you rest your eyes for a moment and calm down you may well remember where you left them. And what's more, when you open your eyes again you can see more clearly. Of course, we can't go round shutting our eyes in the middle of some crisis situation. But at least don't let's make the mistake of looking for God outside the problem or away from it in the peace we look forward to when the problem has been dealt with. He'll be there too. But he's also here now. That, clearly, was one of the things he was saying in sending Jesus into the world. Mary was given clear instructions about what to call her son, Jesus. He was to be called EMMANUEL. Which means 'God with us'.

> Almighty God, it's hard to believe that you're
> around when day by day the world seems to
> get by without you.
> Help me to notice the signs that show there's
> more to things than meets the eye.
> Make me aware of your unseen presence, so
> that when life become specially difficult, or
> specially good, I can be thankful that you are
> there.
>
> *Amen.*

For further reading

Psalm 37:3-9   Wait patiently for the Lord
John 17:20-26   God in us and us in God

JESUS CAME TO EARTH

Corrie Ten Boom was not looking forward to her turn to speak. She was in a ministry team that had gone to a prison to talk about Christ. The team was at one end of a corridor lined with cells and the men peered through the bars to see them. First a woman sang, and the prisoners tried to drown her out with catcalls and boos. Then, when a young man prayed, the noise grew worse. Then it was Corrie. Shouting to be heard, she said: "When I was alone in a cell for 4 months..." Suddenly the corridor grew quiet. Corrie had established a bond with the prisoners. She knew what they were going through. Her time in a World War 2 prison camp made her one of them. They listened. And six of them began to seek Christ. When Jesus came to earth, when he became flesh and lived among us, he became one of us. He understands the suffering, the pain, the rejection that we may be experiencing. He knows your need. He has been there and he cares. In Matthew chapter 11 you can read that he said: "Come to me, all you who labour and are heavy-laden, and I will give you rest." That rest is the peace of God "which passes all understanding".

> O Loving God, thank you for caring so much
>   that you let yourself undergo the experience
>   of human life.
> You have shared our powerlessness and pain, so
>   that you might also share some of your
>   strength and joy with us.
> Come, Lord, and share my life with me today.
> You can, because of what you did in Jesus
>   Christ.
>
> *Amen.*

For further reading

Hebrews 2:18   Jesus understands, from personal experience
1 Peter 2:21-25   Jesus became one of us

JOURNEYS TO BETHLEHEM

Mountain climbing presents a challenge to many people. But to reach the mountain peak may involve different routes. The more direct way taking the shorter steeper climb, or the longer track which takes a more winding way to the summit. Whichever way they take, the climbers reach the same mountain top and experience the view and sense of achievement. At Christmas we are reminded of two groups of people, both of whom are looking for Jesus Christ, the new born king and saviour of the world. The shepherds, guarding their flocks of sheep on the Bethlehem hillside see an angel and then a host of angels telling them of the birth of a saviour. Only a short hurried journey into the town takes them to the cradle where they see Jesus. The other group, the 'wise men from the East' make a longer journey following a star. No doubt they travelled many miles and faced many difficulties. Their journey was only completed when they had found and worshipped Jesus. Like the mountain climbers who took different routes but reached the same mountain peak, so the shepherds and the wise men each had their own journey to make to come to the place of seeing Jesus Christ as king and saviour. And those who truly seek Jesus to-day find him by different routes. Some find him almost in a sudden revelation. For others it can be a long search perhaps taking a lifetime. By whichever way we come, let us this Christmas find the presence of Jesus with us in all our celebrations. He will not disappoint anyone.

> **Lord God, if Jesus Christ is the true light and**
> **the answer to my need, help me to persevere**
> **in seeking for him, so that whether my**
> **journey is to be short or long I may reach the**
> **point where he is no longer just a name, but a**
> **reality.**
> **I ask this in his name.**
> *Amen.*

For further reading

Deuteronomy 4:29-31   Search with all your heart and soul
Luke 2:8-20   The shepherds hurry to Bethlehem

HE IS BESIDE US

I heard a story once about a little boy who, for the first time in his life, was to spend Christmas away from the orphanage. On arriving at his Christmas home he was so bewildered and scared that he rushed into the bedroom and crawled under the nearest bed. From his dark safety he stubbornly refused all calling, pleading and enticing by the mother to come out and join the family. She could, of course, have just caught hold of him and dragged him out, but that wasn't her way. Instead, and in some desperation, she lowered herself down, lay flat on the floor and with much effort squeezed her way under the bed, so that she could lie by the side of the scared little boy. She lay there holding his hand. Her presence was enough. The boy knew that she would meet him on his own level and with that knowledge he was able to come out and join the family. Isn't that what happened that first Christmas? After years of calling, pleading and enticing, when Man stubbornly refused to leave the darkness and join God's family, God had to lower himself down to earth so that he could lie by our sides and meet us at our own level. Just to have his presence, to know that he is beside us enables us to take his hand and take our place in his family.

> Lord, I'm afraid of the Unknown,
>   I'm afraid of you.
> Help me to give you my trust.
> For only by taking the risk can I prove your
>   reality; only by reaching for your hand can I
>   know you are there.
> So help me to give you my trust.
>   *Amen.*

For further reading

Matthew 1:18-25   The birth of the Messiah
John 10:1-15   A place of safety

OBEDIENCE

When we read the Christmas story in the Bible, we can always find something new about it. This year it spoke to me about obedience. First of all, Mary obeyed God by accepting the message that the angel gave to her, that she should bear God's son. Then, Joseph obeyed God, and married Mary in spite of the fact that she was already pregnant. The shepherds too were instantly obedient, when the angels told them to go and find the baby and worship him. So were the wise men. Not one of these people said "No" to God. Each one of them must have had tremendous faith and courage. I wonder what we would have done, if it had been us? How many times have we said "No" to God? We may not have seen any angels bringing us messages, but God speaks to us clearly through the Bible, time and time again. This Christmas let's carry forward the example of the obedience of all these men and women. Let's re-dedicate our lives to him and ask him to help us to be obedient and faithful servants of our Christmas king.

Father, forgive me for all those times when I
have known in my heart what I ought to do,
but have said No, finding an excuse, or
pretending I wasn't sure.
Next time you show me the right way to follow,
or even if now I know it, help me to say Yes,
for the sake of Jesus Christ my Lord.

Amen.

For further reading

Luke 1:26-38   Mary said, "Here am I"
Hebrews 5:8-9   The obedience of Christ

GOD RISKED EVERYTHING

Life, we are told, is a risky business and that's not just true for those who gamble with investments. It's true for everyone who enters relationships, for there's nothing more risky than those. Taking risks, calculated risks, is a real part of life. And giving has always been one such risk. As I think back over Christmas, I recall one lady I knew who only gave to people she anticipated would give her a present in return. Hardly a calculated risk. When I think of the first Christmas, I marvel at the risk God took when he gave of his love in the person of Jesus. "God so loved that he gave," is the way the Bible expresses that giving. The risk God took was the risk of response. Would people respond in gratitude to the generous act of God? Well, as with all gifts, some are grateful, others are not. But loving and giving belong together and are always risky. God did not - does not - give to us only if we give to him. His giving is generous, but if we choose to respond by offering our lives to him we certainly take a risk and we soon discover that self-giving is costly, that entering a loving relationship with God is both a privilege and a responsibility. God risked everything in giving himself to us and we risk everything if we respond. But that's always true of loving relationships. We love because he first loved us. His was the supreme risk.

> **Eternal Lord God, when clouds of doubt shut**
> **out the clear light of your presence, help me**
> **to understand that, while the uncertainties of**
> **faith are great, your trustworthiness is greater**
> **and your faithfulness is above the clouds.**
> *Amen.*

For further reading

Mark 12:41-44   Readiness to give everything
Luke 7:36-50   Lavish love

HE CAME TO SERVE

Did you go to a pantomime at Christmas? I went to see 'Cinderella'. Some times I feel a bit like Cinderella, always having to get up and wait on somebody else. And if a nice prince came along and carried me off, the chances are I'd have to wait on him too! But is this such a bad thing, I wonder? Jesus himself said: " You know that among the Gentiles, those they call their rulers lord it over them, and their great men make their authority felt. Among you this is not to happen. No. Anyone who wants to be great among you must be your servant. And anyone who wants to be first among you must be slave to all. For the Son of Man himself came not to be served, but to serve, and to give his life a ransom for many." What a surprising God we Christians worship.

> **Lord Jesus Christ, your truth turns all our**
> **values upside down.**
> **Your idea of success or failure is the opposite of**
> **ours.**
> **Your way is so different from the way of the**
> **world, you force us to choose between them.**
> **Please give me the courage today to follow**
> **yours.**
>
> *Amen.*

For further reading

Luke 17:7-10   Stern words about service
Luke 22:24-27   But Jesus himself was a servant

THIS IS NOT A GOD-FORSAKEN WORLD

One day in the Christmas period I went into the National Gallery and for a few minutes sat looking at Leonardo da Vinci's picture, 'Virgin of the Rocks'. I found myself gazing in wonder at the face of the virgin looking down adoringly on the face of her son. I saw the young John the Baptist showing recognition of the baby as the Messiah. For me it was a moving experience. I came out into the bustle of Trafalgar Square and as I walked to the tube station I noticed a woman sitting on a doorstep with a battered pram containing what were probably all her possessions. I passed a young man who was begging. I wondered if the tube station would be closed because of 'an incident'. Roads in the West End had been closed earlier in the day. I thought of the refugees in former Yugoslavia. Then I called to mind the picture in the gallery and the major festival we had recently celebrated in church, in honour of the birth of that baby. What I had seen was reality: that in Christ, God has come to share our human life with all its frailties and weakness, and that this is not a God-forsaken world.

Lord Jesus Christ, it's a long time since you
   came to save the world and the world doesn't
   seem to be getting any better.
But you are no dictator, and you deal with
   human beings one by one.
Change that fraction of the world I call 'myself',
   that my life, focused on you in grateful love,
   may draw the eyes of others to recognize you
   as Saviour and Lord.

Amen.

For further reading

Isaiah 61:1-4   He was sent to bind up the broken-hearted
Luke 2:1-7   No room in the inn

VULNERABLE GOD

Christmas was given extra meaning for us this year by the presence of our first grand-child, Rebecca. I never cease to be amazed by the miracle of new birth, and at the utter dependency of a baby on others for everything needed for survival. Having Rebecca with us this Christmas reminded me even more strikingly than usual just what God did at the first Christmas. He himself, the creator of the universe, became, in Christ, a baby, just as dependent on human beings like ourselves as our grand-daughter is. In fact he made himself far more vulnerable than to-day's babies. That all happened 2000 years ago, of course. But if the birth of Jesus shows us how God works, then we have to face the staggering fact that he may still be depending on us to-day. Love cannot exist in isolation, and since God is love, his very existence may depend on us responding to his love for us. It's a terrifying thought that God may have given the future of the universe into our hands. We all know in our hearts of the immense power love has to overcome all adversity, and the terrible suffering caused when love is rejected. Most of us are not very good at loving, but let's try and share what love we have in the year that's nearly here, and by doing so respond to God's love for us. Our very existence may depend on it.

> Eternal Father, compared with your vast love
> my love for you and for others is like a
> flickering candle in the full blaze of the sun.
> Yet you call for my partnership in bringing the
> light of love into the world.
> I offer today my bit of loving for you to enlarge
> it and use it as you will, in the name of Jesus
> Christ.
> *Amen.*

For further reading

Matthew 22:37-40   Love the Lord your God with all your heart
1 Corinthians 13:1-13   If I have no love, I am nothing

COMFORTABLE WORLD

Shortly before Christmas I went to hear Kings Church in Shenfield perform Graham Kendrick's "Make way for Christmas" - a joyful, musical celebration of the holy birth. Sitting back comfortably in my seat, I was suddenly taken aback by a line that leapt out at me: "There is no danger from the Christ child in the manger." Christmas is comfortable: the baby Jesus, the angels, the shepherds and kings, the carols. It gives us a warm feeling. People who wouldn't normally go near a church go to a carol service at Christmas. Perhaps a modern interpretation like I heard or the more traditional nine lessons and carols. Quite simply, it's OK to be seen to be a Christian at Christmas. But like all children, the Christ child grew up. He grew up and said and did things that made the community around him feel uncomfortable and even threatened because he challenged their ways of living and their attitudes to one another. Here in Brentwood our community is being challenged too. There are very important issues that have to be resolved. We all know about the poverty, the unemployment and the violence in our country, and even in our own local community. But there are other issues too. As individuals we have to decide whether to work on Sundays, whether to shop on Sundays, whether to turn a blind eye to things that aren't quite honest, whether to let our Christian standards slip. Will you be making a stand for Christ in the year to come, or are you happy to leave the Christ child comfortably in the manger?

> **O Living Christ, how do you put up with such
> easy-going, childish followers as I have been?
> Give me more of your Spirit.
> Show me, today, some point on which to take
> my stand for your truth and love against the
> values of the world; and give me your
> courage and your grace to do as you would
> do, for the sake of your Kingdom.**
>
> *Amen.*

For further reading

Daniel 6:6-24   Daniel making a stand
Luke 16:10-15   People of integrity

COMFORTABLE WORLD

I've no idea how much you know about these microchip things that go in a computer. I know very little about them, but I do know that they seem to have a power out of all proportion to their size. Some of them are so small you need a microscope to see them, and yet they can control aeroplanes and even spaceships. Over the Christmas period we have been celebrating an event which had an effect out of all proportion to its size. The birth of a baby in the one-eyed town of Bethlehem 2000 years ago doesn't seem very important. And yet that baby was God himself, the creator of the universe, come amongst his created people. And his spirit has remained with us throughout the years to this day, able to lighten the darkness of our lives just as a torch can flood a path on a winter's evening. As we set out towards yet another new year with all its uncertainties we can be sure that the love of God revealed so long ago in the birth of Jesus will always be with us, available if we call on him in prayer. So, in the words of that lovely Christmas carol: "O little town of Bethlehem, the hopes and fears of all the years are met in you tonight".

Lord Jesus Christ, when I feel too insignificant
and unqualified to make any difference, help
me to remember how small and helpless you
were, in the manger and on the cross, yet you
have changed the world.
Give us strength to join our littleness with
yours and, in your company, to go on
changing the world, until God's kingdom
comes.

Amen.

For further reading

Luke 2:25-33   Simeon recognises the significance of the baby
Matthew 28:20   I am with you always

CLOSING MESSAGES

NO NEED TO BE CLEVER

I phoned my brother yesterday! Nothing very unusual in that, you may be thinking. No. But my brother lives in Barbados. And I have to admit, I've never got over the miracle of the fact that he can sit in his armchair in his home on the other side of the Atlantic and chat to me in London. Of course, I accept that plenty of people do understand the technology that has made this possible. But I for one don't. But that doesn't stop me phoning him. And it doesn't stop me getting excited when I hear his voice. I suppose Christian faith is a bit like that. Having a relationship with someone apparently far away but actually very near. But so many of us are not prepared to let go and believe in that miracle, the miracle of talking to God, sensing that he is near, because we don't understand how it can be. We think we're not clever enough to understand and that somehow if you don't understand then it can't happen. One of my favourite verses in the Bible is in a letter St. Paul wrote to a new church in Corinth. "It isn't human cleverness," he said, "that will bring us close to God. It's a willingness to do what many people might consider foolish. It's a willingness to accept that Jesus has shown us by dying on the cross that God loves us as - well - foolishly as that!" And so we can trust him to hear us when we talk to him, and to answer us in ways we'll understand.

> Sometimes I feel silly talking to you like this,
> God.
> Sometimes I'm not sure that you're listening to
> what I say.
> Then in the stillness, when I'm finished, my
> heart hears you reply.

For further reading

Hebrews 11:6-7; 23-27   Great faith in the invisible God
1 Peter 1:8-10   You have not seen him, yet you loved him

SO WONDERFUL

When we get together to record our messages for the telephone, I've often noticed that the speakers tend to speed up their rate of delivery. They get quicker and quicker. I know, I do it too! But you see, it's just that we feel we've got something wonderful to say, about God's love, and Jesus Christ's sacrifice on the cross, and the joy of the fellowship of the Holy Spirit. But we've got less than two minutes in which to say it! What I would like to get across now is that God has all the time in the world to listen to you. His timescale is very different from ours. "A thousand ages in his sight are like an evening gone". So, if you have been considering turning to God, through his son, please don't put it off any longer. Tell him of your fears and hopes, your joys and troubles, and then be quiet and hear him, the still small voice of the God who made you and loves you.

> I'm waiting for the moment when we can talk:
>   when the children are quiet;
>   when there's nothing on TV;
>   when I'm not so busy;
>   when there's nothing else to do.
> You've got to help me, God, make space for you.

For further reading

Psalm 145:1-15   Something so wonderful to say
2 Corinthians 13:14   But less than two minutes to say it

DOUBT AND FAITH

I heard this recently: " If someone said to me, 'I don't have any doubts,' I would say to them, 'You don't know what it is to have faith!" Does that cheer you? I thought it was comforting and encouraging, for most people who want to believe in the Christian faith are at times worried by doubts or they go on so far and then comes trouble and in come the doubts too. Or illness comes and doubts start swarming in. As someone said to me whose faith is being tried now, "Faith is continuing, holding on, losing and finding it again. There is no easy answer. You have to think and battle, sometimes just to weigh anchor and let the storm blow over you." But remember that the dear Lord is there, strong, unchangeable, however much our faith wavers. He has said, " I am the Lord. I change not. I have loved you with an everlasting love." So, when doubts come over us, let us turn to God, our rock, as the man who wrote Psalm 39 said, "I waited, I waited for the Lord and he stooped down to me. He heard my cry, he drew me from the deadly pit, from the miry clay, he set my feet upon a rock." Christ is our rock, as many people down the years have proved.

> I know what doubt is:
>> I'm not sure about faith.
> I know what betrayal is:
>> I'm not sure about trust.
> I know what fear is:
>> I'm not sure about love.
> Help me know less of the world I've got,
>> and more of your Kingdom to come.

For further reading

2 Corinthians 12:7-10   Power comes to its full strength in weakness
1 Peter 1:7   Faith which stands the test

THE MESSAGE DOESN'T CHANGE

Do you like things to change, or do you prefer to keep life simple, going on in the same old way? I hate change myself, and it takes me ages to make up my mind to do something different. I've been doing these talks for MESSAGE for over ten years now, and the fact is that just about everything has changed since then, like it or not. I've moved house, changed my job, and after much careful thought I even got married! The producers and editors of MESSAGE have changed and no longer can I drive through Ilford Town Centre to deliver the master tapes: they've pedestrianised it all! Really, the only thing that has not changed is our message itself. Ten years ago our message was: "God can be trusted. Whatever the future holds, God does not alter." Now, ten years later, we say it is still true, and God has proved it. And our message will be the same for all the future ahead of us. There is a famous hymn that says it far better than I can:

> "Great is thy faithfulness, oh God my Father,
> There is no shadow of turning with thee.
> Thou changest not, thy compassions they fail not:
> As thou hast been thou for ever wilt be".

> It seemed so important at the time, Lord,
> why I had no time for you.
> My life was full of other things:
> demands; pressures; worries.
> I didn't want to bother you.
> Then someone said you'd missed me,
> and hoped to see me back.
> They told me what you've done for me.
> I didn't know you cared so much.

For further reading

James 1:16-17 With God there is no variableness or shadow of turning
Revelation 1:8 Alpha and Omega

INDEX TO KEY WORDS

INDEX TO SCRIPTURE REFERENCES

ABOUT MESSAGE...

MESSAGE was started in 1969 by the late Norah Coggan, sister of the then Archbishop of Canterbury Lord Donald Coggan. In the intervening years over half a million people have been helped through just listening to the personal, Christian experiences of local script writers and recorders.

The need for such a service is no greater than now, in the present day, when all the stresses and strains of personal, business and family life are becoming intolerable for some people.

MESSAGE could offer just those particular words of comfort and hope that callers may need. The telephone number given at the end of the message offers an opportunity to speak to someone personally should the caller desire. Callers need not give their names unless they wish as the service is completely anonymous and confidential.

MESSAGE is a 24-hour 'Dial and Listen' telephone service relating the Bible to everyday situations.

Scripts are written and recorded by local Christians of all denominations. The two minute recorded messages are available at local call charges from 11 Centres throughout the UK. MESSAGE is not a Premium Rate Service. Its telephone numbers can be found in local telephone directories under 'MESSAGE'. Most Centres offer a further telephone number for callers who want to speak to someone personally.

MESSAGE is a practical way of sharing the good news of Jesus Christ revealed in the Bible. It is a modern ministry supported throughout by prayer, presenting the Gospel in terms of personal thought and experience. MESSAGE is an ever expanding network of local Centres (fully supported by a national resource for administration, publicity material and advice) able to respond to local situations to give help and comfort in times of need. We believe it is God's work in which all Christians can be involved.

The National Committee would be pleased to arrange for someone to visit you initially to tell you more about MESSAGE. It also has a team of visiting speakers, most of whom are directly concerned in running Centres who would be happy to approach local Councils of Churches or "Churches Together" to organise exploratory meetings etc.

MESSAGE is a Registered Charity, No. 297409.

ABOUT THE BIBLE READING FELLOWSHIP

In November 1921 a woman in the congregation of St Matthew's Church, Brixton, London said to her vicar: "We in the pews need help with our Bible reading, our prayer and our Holy Communion." Challenged by this the vicar, The Revd Leslie Mannering, wrote in his parish magazine in December 1921 "Why not have a great parochial fellowship for the purpose of deepening the life of Bible reading, prayer and Holy Communion in each of us. We shall make the venture, believing God has called us to this."

The first leaflet of daily Bible readings, written by Leslie Mannering, was produced in January 1922. Others beyond St Matthews heard about the notes and began to request them for use in their churches, and so began The Bible Reading Fellowship. As a Registered Charity (No. 233280) BRF's stated objective is to stimulate and encourage people to read, value, understand and enjoy the message of the Bible.

In addition to a wide range of books and group Bible study resources, BRF publishes two regular series of Bible reading notes - *New Daylight* and *Guidelines*. These are published three times a year (in January, May and September).

New Daylight provides a pattern for daily Bible reading. Each day's reading contains a Bible passage (printed out in full, from the version chosen by the contributor), along with a brief commentary and explanation, and a suggestion for prayer, meditation or reflection. The sections of commentary often draw on and reflect the experiences of the contributors themselves and thus offer contemporary and personal insights into the readings. Sunday readings focus on the themes of prayer and Holy Communion.

Guidelines contains running commentary, with introductions and background information, arranged in weekly units. Each week's material is usually broken up into at least six sections. Readers can take as much or as little at a time as they wish. The whole 'week' can be used at a sitting, or split up into convenient parts. This flexible arrangement allows for one section to be used each weekday. A Bible will be needed. The last section of each week is usually called 'Guidelines' and has points for thought, meditation and prayer. A short list of books, to help with further reading, appears at the end of some contributions.

Both *New Daylight* and *Guidelines* may be obtained from your local Christian bookshop or by subscription direct from BRF.

Readers of BRF notes are to be found today in 60 countries worldwide. Among those who write regularly for the notes are Adrian Plass, Joyce Huggett, Rosemary Green, David Winter, Gerard W. Hughes and Henry Wansbrough.

For more information about the notes, and the full range of BRF publications, write to: BRF, Peter's Way, Sandy Lane West, Oxford OX4 5HG (tel: 01865 748227).